T0146670

NEVER ENOUGH
LOVE

JOHN LAZANO

authorHOUSE®

AuthorHouse™
1663 Liberty Drive
Bloomington, IN 47403
www.authorhouse.com
Phone: 1 (800) 839-8640

Published by AuthorHouse 11/05/2018

ISBN: 978-1-5462-4242-0 (sc)
ISBN: 978-1-5462-4241-3 (e)

Library of Congress Control Number: 2018905850

Print information available on the last page.

This book is printed on acid-free paper.

Never Enough Love

An Amazing True-Life Story of Family, Traveling the World,
Adventure, Romance, Deception & Consequences

By John Lazano

This book is dedicated in loving memory to Steven Brancale,
whose short life inspired me to live mine to the fullest

TABLE OF CONTENTS

PROLOGUE

Driving down Las Vegas Boulevard, I couldn't believe it was 2018. I was 65 years old and feeling reflective as I passed the digital billboards and magnificent hotels on the Strip. The Wynn, the Venetian, the Palazzo, the Mirage, Caesars Palace—was Celine Dion still performing at the Colosseum? I guess so, but I thought she'd retired after her husband had passed away. Apparently I was wrong.

The Bellagio with its spectacular, synchronized water show and all the other attractions—no matter how many times I drove up and down the Strip, this place never failed to amaze me. Even after living here for over 12 years, Las Vegas was in a never-ending state of transformation. There was always something new to do or a sensational attraction coming that would be exciting to anticipate. The last few years had been especially dramatic with all the new construction and now the addition of professional sports. The Golden Knights and soon the Las Vegas Raiders football team, including a fantastic new stadium—the city was exploding in all directions. This town was the last stop on the train for me.

As I passed the Mandalay Bay, my heart sank. How could anyone forget what happened on October 1, 2017? The mass shooting had left 58 dead and over 500 injured. It was a terrible tragedy that will always be remembered as one of the darkest days in Las Vegas history.

As I looked to my left, I saw the Little Chapel of the West, the church where Elvis and Ann-Margret got married at the end of *Viva Las*

Vegas, back in 1963. It's now a historical landmark and I have stood in its doorway many times, just to say I was right in the spot where Elvis married Ann-Margret. They probably should have gotten together in real life, but that's another story.

I turned on the radio and was flipping around when I hit Sirius and "Cousin Brucie" came on the air. Bruce Morrow was a famous radio disc jockey from the early 1960s. When he was at WABC AM radio in New York, he and a fellow DJ named Murray the K (Kaufman) were the most important people in radio. "Cousin Brucie" was responsible for helping launch the Four Seasons and many other singing groups at that time, most coming from the New York metropolitan area. Murray the K had a show called the "The Swingin' Soiree," broadcasting from 1010 WINS, another popular station in New York, and he and Brucie had a competition going on. Murray was friends with the Beatles and had them on his radio show, first by telephone the morning after they arrived in the USA, then doing a live broadcast from the Plaza Hotel, where they were staying before their appearance on the *Ed Sullivan Show*. Murray was referred to as "the Fifth Beatle" by George Harrison because of his long association and friendship with the group. Murray the K died in 1982 at the age of 60, but was considered to be the number one disc jockey on New York radio for a majority of the 1960s.

It was amazing to think that his main rival, "Cousin Brucie," was still on the air at 82, spinning the oldies. His voice sounded the same as it did way back then.

Brucie came on the radio and said, "Cousins, let me tell ya a little story about our next song. Did you know that a struggling, unknown song writer named Jerry Fuller wrote 'Travelin' Man' while waiting to pick up his wife from work back in 1961? He actually wrote the song by pounding it out on the dashboard of his car. He couldn't play the guitar and wrote the words down on a paper napkin he had with him. His intention was to write the song for Sam Cooke. The next day he took the rough idea of the song into the studio, where he and Glen Campbell and a fellow named Dave Burgess recorded a demo of it. Jerry took it to Sam Cooke's manager, J.W. Alexander, and asked him to listen to it. He said he would and that was the last Jerry heard of it, at least for a while.

"Sam Cooke's manager listened to part of it, didn't like it and decided to throw it in the trash can. In the next office, however, was Ricky Nelson's bass player, Joe Osborn. Joe heard it through the wall and came around the corner and asked J.W. what had he just played. Could he hear it again? J.W. said it was in the trash and he could have it. Joe took the song to Ricky Nelson. Ricky loved it so much that he did a full recording of it using the Jordanaires as backup. Ricky had to ask Elvis Presley if he could use the Jordanaires, who were his primary backup group.

"They made a few minor changes and then called Jerry Fuller. Jerry had never heard of Joe Osborn and was completely surprised he had taken the discarded record to Ricky Nelson and he had re-recorded it. They asked Jerry if he had any more songs. He said he had about eighty of them, then went on to write several of Rick Nelson's most famous hits, 'Young World' and 'It's up to You,' just to name a few. From the trash pail to a national hit! Can you imagine the odds of that happening? This was the true meaning of the word 'serendipity.'

"'Travelin' Man' went Number One six weeks after its release during May of 1961 and Jerry Fuller went on to become a sought—after composer and songwriter with many top 20 hits under his belt.

"Shortly thereafter, Ozzie Nelson, Ricky's dad, got the idea to superimpose travel backgrounds into the performance while Rick was playing. Thus, the first music video was created. This clip was just put into the Smithsonian as the first official music video made in history! Now, let's play 'Travelin' Man' for all my cousins…"

The song came on and I couldn't believe just how influential it had been and what an impact it had had on my life. It was uncanny…

I began to think back to where I had come from and everything that had happened—boy, what an incredible journey it had been! Even now, as I look back after everything that occurred, I'm not sure how it will end up. I can only tell you what took place and yes, it's all true!

The names have been changed to protect the innocent, as well as the guilty…and that includes me…

CHAPTER 1

I suppose being from the Bronx had its advantages, from the famous restaurants, delicatessens, flower shops and Italian bakeries on Arthur Avenue, to the colorful books that have been written and movies that have been made about the gangsters, singing groups, and entertainers that grew up there. For those who don't know, Arthur Avenue was the "Park Avenue" of the Bronx in those days. I was too young to know any better and these were only stories I heard at family gatherings years after we moved away. It seemed that every Italian family had a member they claimed was in the mafia or had a close connection to someone who was. The family bragged about it. It basically meant, "don't anybody mess with us," or the "boys" would "take care" of you. To this day, I still question if any of this was true.

There was also a relative who was an undertaker and a cousin who was gay. The gay cousin's sexual proclivity was kept a family secret until he was old enough to move away. In later years if his name ever did come up, my aunt and uncle would say he was "doing fine" and there was no more discussion after that.

In my family it was Uncle George, who supposedly was connected to the mob in the 1930s. As the story goes, my aunt married him when she was 18 and he was 45. She did it so the family would not starve during the Great Depression. Apparently he was abusive to my aunt and ran prostitutes and booze during prohibition. From what my mother told me, my aunt put up with it because they always had food, gifts for Christmas, and never had to go on "Home Relief," which was like welfare as we know it today. This was a big deal in those days. In the late 50s when we went to my aunt's apartment to eat, Uncle George was there, sitting at the head of the table very quietly. He would say grace and if someone asked him what he did when he worked, he said he was a "barber." When he died, they gave a long eulogy in church about what a wonderful man he had been in his life. Oh, really?

"Frankie Oreo"—he was the undertaker. If anyone died, the family called Cousin Frankie. He picked up the body, embalmed it, then either brought it back to the house to be laid out in the living room, or to his funeral parlor in Harlem for the viewing. He also made arrangements for the flowers, limos, and even the food after the funeral. He had the real "racket" going on. After he died, his daughter took over, eventually selling out to a large chain of funeral homes with multiple locations throughout the city. When Frankie was alive, he always said everyone was going to die sooner or later, so he and his daughter would never run out of "customers." The rumor was that she got several million dollars for the business, retired, and moved to Florida. I guess he was right!

I came screaming into this world at Jacobi Hospital on Pelham Parkway in November of 1952. I had the standard ten fingers and ten toes, although my father did tell me that when he first saw me, my head looked like a stretched out sausage and didn't look normal. My poor mother suffered in labor for 14 hours, until they decided to use forceps to get me out, thus explaining the elongated noggin. Every time she told the story about giving birth to me, it included a dissertation about the forceps, her episiotomy, the 28 stitches she needed, and then how she sat in a "sitz bath" for three weeks healing up. Over the years, I heard this same story in detail, hundreds of times until she died. It was her way of telling me and anyone else who would listen, what she had to go through for her one and only "prodigal" son. This is how lifelong "Italian Guilt" begins—with forceps, an episiotomy, 28 stitches, and a sitz bath! It turns an Italian son into an indentured servant to his mother for the rest of his life. If you are from an Italian family, you know exactly what I mean...

My parents were first generation Americans, born to poor Italian immigrants that came right off the boat from the old country. Word got back to the family in Italy that the streets of New York were lined with gold. The thought of a different world, riches and a new life, prompted many of them to buy one-way ocean liner tickets to the United States, in what was known as steerage class to get across the ocean. This was a horrible seven- to ten-day voyage in the bottom of the ship.

Many of the travelers left with only the clothes on their backs and a small bag. Many had a sponsor or someone who they would live with, but many came by themselves and weren't sure where they would end up. It took guts, and my relatives were all part of this mass migration from Europe to America.

My grandmother Carmella and her sister Zitzi made the voyage and were the first ones that did. They could not speak a word of English, but my great-grandparents sent them anyway. When they arrived they were processed through Ellis Island, and then went to live with a cousin in Harlem, who had already been in America for over ten years. Who knows if they were really cousins or not? Everyone was called cousin. They both became seamstresses and eventually my grandmother married a barber and had eight children, while Zitzi never married and lived with my grandparents until she died. That was the way it was in those days.

These New York melting pots were mainly Italian, Irish, and Jewish. The Irish and Italians did the manual labor such as bricklaying and construction, while many of the Jewish people began to work in the garment industry. In spite of the difficult and uncomfortable passage they made coming to the United States, they all managed to settle down, have families and create the ethnic neighborhoods that New York City and its five boroughs are famous for.

After World War II ended, my mother and father—like many couples—were matched up and, after a few months of supervised dating, were married in a traditional Italian wedding. My mother was the youngest of eight children and the baby in her family. Like all women from that era, she was a virgin when she got married and my father was the only man she was ever with. As a matter of fact, she was so modest that other than giving birth to my sister and me, she would never go to an OB/GYN or get a pap smear during her entire life because at that time the doctors were all men.

When my parents moved out after living with my grandmother for four years in Harlem, they settled in the Bronx and lived off Pelham Parkway, which at the time was considered to be an upscale neighborhood. For my mother, getting married and leaving home was a big deal, but moving out of the apartment to the Bronx was traumatic! Eventually her whole family followed her and ended up on White Plains Road, which was not far away.

I was told when I was a baby, my father would walk me in the stroller around the neighborhood accompanied by Jake LaMotta the famous boxer, portrayed by Robert DeNiro in the movie *"Raging Bull"*. My parents moved in right next door to him and didn't even know it. Dad would see him in his backyard and go over and watch him practice punching the bag.

In those days, if you were Italian and lived next to another Italian, you became friends. Jake and dad became fast friends and on weekends would go horseback riding at the stables in the middle of Pelham Parkway and took me along because I liked to pet the horses.

Jake and his family moved away not too long after we moved in. He was becoming more famous and you know how it goes with fame and fortune.

Pelham Parkway was a beautiful, tree-lined boulevard and in the Bronx at that time, it was like being in the country. I recall as a child whenever we went back to visit the old neighborhood in the springtime it was always sunny, no smog, with the scent of flowers and horse manure that you could smell when the wind blew in the right direction.

A little before I turned two, we moved out to Bellmore, Long Island, where we started our middle-class life in postwar, suburban America. Many young couples living in the Bronx, Brooklyn or Queens were making their way out of the city to give their children a new life and my parents were part of that pilgrimage out to the new suburbs.

The Southern State Parkway was moving east, automobiles were improving and service on the Long Island Railroad in and out of the city was becoming more reliable, so why not? Levitt & Sons started the first tract home community in the late 1940s, called Levittown, where a GI could purchase a home for $5995 and get a mortgage for it on the newly established GI Bill.

My mother's family, back on White Plains Road, were in tears at the thought of her moving away again, but my father was determined to get us out to the country to give us a better life. He managed to get a job with a printing company, eventually joining the "Amalgamated Lithographers of America." Now he was a union man and would always have a job with benefits and could never get fired.

He worked his way up from being paper handler to pressman, and then got into management, which meant more money for our family. All the printing shops were located in the city and he took the Long Island Railroad from the Bellmore Station into Manhattan every day, never missing a day of work for years. Even in the blizzard of 1956, he walked three miles to the train station to be on time. He made it there, but the train never arrived and he walked back home.

Something I will never forget was when I was three years old. We would go to the train station every Sunday to purchase his weekly ticket. It was October of 1955 and the last of the great steam engines that the Long Island Railroad used was going to come through the station for the final time and he wanted me to see it. I looked down the tracks from the platform and saw the plume of smoke coming down the tracks. It scared the hell out of me, so much so, that I ran and hid in the station until it passed and didn't see a thing. I only remember feeling the ground shake as the thunderous locomotive passed through the station. It felt and seemed like a giant fire-breathing dragon to me as a young child.

That same month and year, my sister Debbie was born in Bay Shore at Southside Hospital. Suddenly, our little Cape Cod house seemed pretty small. My sister and I had to share a room and when she woke up screaming, so did I. I remember her in the carriage, with me holding my mother's one free hand, while we walked three blocks to the grocery store on Jerusalem Ave.

Like all mothers during this era, she was a stay-at-home mom who got up early, made my father breakfast before he left for the train station at 4:30 AM every morning and took care of my sister and me all day. She had food on the table for him when he came through the door dead tired, smelling of printer's ink, every evening at 7:30 PM.

When he came in, I hugged him with his coat still on and he smelled just like New York City. Anyone from New York knows the unmistakable scent that the city has and how it sticks to your clothing. It was cold, a little smoky, and that combined with the smell of the ink made the scent very distinctive. His fingernails were always dirty from working with ink all day, and every Saturday he made sure he scrubbed them clean for the weekend.

From the time I was four, I remember mother's homemade Italian sauce that she'd slave over from five in the morning until it was served at our traditional dinner at one PM every Sunday. Spaghetti and meatballs, eggplant or baked ziti, with my father drinking Schlitz beer. After dinner my parents took my sister and me for a ride to Carvel for ice cream.

Carvel was the first soft-serve ice cream in the country, and it was the best! I loved a large vanilla cone, especially when it began to melt. I would have to lick it on the sides, all the way around, quickly, so it wouldn't drip all over me. As it melted, it would soften the cake cone so I could bite right into it. It was delicious and creamy. My sister and I always wanted seconds but my parents said, "No! You two had enough!" Oh well, couldn't hurt to try.

When my father left for work at 4:30 AM, we would all stay up and watch the *Jimmy Dean Show* that came on at 5:00 AM every weekday morning. During the day my mother would read me *Tales of the Arabian Nights,* let me watch cartoons in the morning, eat baloney sandwiches for lunch, take a nap and then when I woke up, the *"Mickey Mouse Club"* would come on the Philco 21-inch, blonde television set that we had. Even though I was only five, I was in love with "Annette." She was and always will be my favorite *"Mouseketeer."*

On Saturdays my sister and I would watch *The Lone Ranger, Mighty Mouse, Hop along Cassidy, Sky King,* and then *My Friend Flicka.* In the afternoon, my father would take us food shopping at Hills Supermarket, so we would be out of my mother's hair and she could clean the house. I had a very secure, traditional Italian upbringing.

When I turned five, I started kindergarten at Jacob Gunther Elementary School and went to St. Rayfield's Catholic Church in East

Meadow. It was the largest Catholic Church in that community and everyone from the neighborhood went there. The priests were young and handsome and I could see that many of the women who attended Mass had crushes on them. After each Sunday service, they all wanted to talk to this one or that one. It was a real show.

I was in Catechism school to prepare me for First Communion. The school was part of the church and had uncomfortable wooden benches. Father Michael was the young, up-and-coming priest who was going to take over the parish. Everyone loved him and he gave the sermon on Sundays. Father Michael turned out to be a pedophile. Some kid snitched on him and the powers-that-be removed him from the parish and transferred him. That is what they did in those days. No one said a word about why or what. He was just gone.

One of my church friends, Albert Bosco, nicknamed "Albi," would make me laugh out loud. The Dominican Sisters would come over and hit us with a ruler across the knuckles whenever they caught us fooling around. The sisters once showed me a completed circle and then said, "This is God, no beginning and no end."

I looked at it, then her, and said, "It doesn't make any sense to me." She slapped me across the face! I knew then it was about blind faith. Since I always questioned everything, church wasn't for me. Regardless, I always had a deep belief in Jesus and the Holy Mother. Sundays, however, had one saving grace. During our family sit-down dinner at one PM, I would always get a shot glass full of beer while my dad had his. This routine of going to church, school, and being around my family continued throughout the 1950s until the end of the decade. I was in fourth grade at Jacob Gunther when things began to change.

I specifically remember watching *Ozzie and Harriet* on TV in April of 1961, when Ricky Nelson sang "Travelin' Man" for the first time. After the first version, he sang it again with a travelogue superimposed behind him. I was mesmerized and I turned to my mother and said, "Mom, I want to be just like him."

We had been in our little Cape Cod house in Bellmore for almost ten years and now there was a new push to go east again out on Long Island. One Sunday my father was thumbing through the newspaper then took off driving thirty miles out to Commack to look at a new development called Pine Cone Woods. He put a deposit on the lot and came home in time for Sunday dinner. He announced at dinner that he had bought another house. My mother was furious, but went along with the program, as most women did then. She said she wanted to see it that day, and as soon as we were done eating, we all went for a ride to see the "new house." Once my mother saw it, she fell in love with it and our little house in Bellmore went up for sale.

We moved to Commack in the winter of 1962, before the Long Island Expressway had reached Route 110 in Huntington. Back then, Commack was considered to be the end of the world, a mere forty-six miles from New York City. I was nine when we bought the house. It took eight months to build and was on a quarter of an acre like all the other cookie-cutter homes. I think the home cost my father $18,500. He used his GI Bill again and was approved in a matter of days with no money down.

You either got a ranch, high ranch, or a colonial. My parents chose the high ranch; my mother did have a say in that. The upper level contained a kitchen, a living room, dining room, two full bathrooms, and three bedrooms.

Downstairs contained a den, bedroom, a half bath, a laundry room, and a two-car garage. This house was the personification of the American Dream in 1962. We had a chocolate brown, four door, 1959 Ford Galaxy 500 with clear slipcovers on the upholstery that you could barely sit on when it was hot. Back then, common car color choices were often flat brown or an ugly green, with no clear coat. Can you imagine that? The hood, roof and trunk would fade after their first hot and humid summer on Long Island.

Our block was lined with Chevys, Fords, Oldsmobiles, and Cadillacs, which the so-called Mafia guys drove. Everyone deliberately left their cars outside so all the neighbors could see how well they were doing. My father was friends with them and always wanted to be on their good side in case he needed a favor. Supposedly, on several occasions they helped him; at least that is what I overheard him telling my mother. Who knows?

I will never forget that in the summer of '63 I went on a church trip to the original Yankee Stadium to see a baseball game. After the game, we met all the Yankees. Yes, the real "Boys of Summer" which included meeting Mickey Mantle and the rest of the famous players. Little did I know how important a historical event this was. I even had a baseball signed by the whole team. I traded it to another kid, Pete Geossi, for some other team's baseball cards. I don't remember why. If I had kept the ball, it would have been worth a fortune.

Years later, I heard that Peter ran away and joined the Moonies. It devastated both his father and mother because he was always a clean-cut, conservative kid that stayed close to home and had a real passion for baseball. Finally, he came to his senses and left the cult, had a family, and returned to a normal life. Most recently, I found out he was a retired bus driver living a quiet life in Baltimore.

The Murattino family moved in three houses away and our families became friends right away. Joe, the father, purchased the first color TV on the block in 1964 and Joe's family owned Town & County Cement. He was supposedly in the Mafia and was like the "Godfather" on the block. I was friends with Ricky, his son. He was the first kid in the neighborhood I met when I moved in. We would go over to Joe's house on Sunday to watch Walt Disney's, *"The Wonderful World of Color."* All the television sets back then were either RCA Victor—remember their logo with the dog sitting on top of the phonograph?—Emerson, or GE, all made in the USA. His wife, Betty would cook a big Italian dinner and we all would eat at the dining room table. After dinner the adults would play cards and the kids would watch TV.

After we left Joe's house we went home and turned on the *Ed Sullivan Show*. It was in black and white, but the best variety show of the time. Sullivan had every performer, act, or group on his show that was hot in the country at the time. Usually it was their first appearance on national TV. Right after that they became famous, literally overnight. I watched it most of the time, but sometimes I fell asleep because school was early the next morning. Although I did see Elvis and the Beatles as they shot to stardom after they performed on that famous stage located at 1697 Broadway, which is now known as the Ed Sullivan Theater, now a treasured historic landmark in New York City.

Every Sunday morning and on holidays we drove back to the Bronx to see my grandmother, my mother's mother, who still lived in the same apartment on White Plains Road, then go over and see my father's mother, who lived near the Grand Concourse. We did this as a family until I was 15. I hated to go sometimes, but had to…

Growing up, I was a shy, introverted kid, and I'd often spend time in my bedroom singing along with 45 RPM records, writing poetry at the dining room table, or I'd practice my guitar out on the front stoop of our home. I learned to play the guitar at nine when I was going into fifth grade. Because I was shy about being in a new school, I got into music, writing songs and working on my poems. I got a music book called *Alfred's Chord Fingering Dictionary* and learned to play a few standard chords. It got me good enough to accompany myself on the guitar when I was singing.

By 1963, however, the British Invasion hit the US and Rick Nelson and Elvis were fading fast as the Brits took over the airwaves. Now I was beginning to hit puberty and my awareness of sex wasn't far behind.

Toward the end of fifth grade, my friends and I would find *Playboy* magazines in the woods or we'd pay an older kid to buy them for us, then, as a group, we'd whack off in the woods. The first time I jacked off, a big drop of cum came out of the tip of my dick and I didn't know what it was, so I started crying. Because I was pulling on my pecker so hard I was sure I had broken something inside me. I also thought I had committed an irreversible mortal sin and was surely going to Hell! I felt that I had done something terribly wrong and was tainted for life. Although, I must admit, it did feel pretty good after I got used to doing it a couple of times.

I remember the Cuban Missile Crisis in 1962, the October after we had moved in. We'd have to do drills in school where we'd get under our desks and put our hands over our heads—like that would protect anyone from anything. Most of my friends believed Russia was going to attack us and were scared to death.

I will never forget Frank McGee, Walter Cronkite, Chet Huntley, and David Brinkley, who were the anchors for NBC News at the time. Everyone would gather around their 19-inch TVs every evening during the crisis as it unfolded. Night after night, our beloved President Kennedy would address the nation, giving us an update and saying the US was prepared to use nuclear warheads against Cuba and Russia if we had to. Everyone was scared out of their minds and, as we all remember, at the last minute the crisis was averted when Nikita Khrushchev backed down and the Russian ships turned around. The young American president was now a hero for standing up and bringing us back from the brink of nuclear war.

The next year in November of 1963, much to the shock of the nation and the world, Kennedy was assassinated and Lyndon Johnson became the next president. I remember it to this day. It was a Friday at about two-thirty in the afternoon New York time. I was in sixth grade, in gym class when the announcement came over the loudspeaker that the president had been killed. The teachers all broke down and everyone was in a panic, grief-stricken and in disbelief. They sent all of us home early and we watched the whole thing on TV for days as the nation and the world mourned, right before our eyes. The new president, LBJ, was sworn in on the plane back to Washington, but no one wanted to believe that the young, vibrant, American president was really dead.

The nation's heartfelt sorrow was palpable and if you were alive, it is something you will never forget.

In 1964, I was twelve and wasn't sure what I wanted to be or do when I grew up. One afternoon my mother took me to the matinee at the local theater like we always did on Saturdays. We went to see an Elvis double feature, *Roustabout* and *Kissin' Cousins*. She bought me Cracker Jacks before the show. Once we were seated, I opened the box which back then was lined with wax to prevent the Cracker Jacks from sticking to the inside of the cardboard box when the weather was hot.

The prizes inside the box were pretty good and there was actually some value to them. It might be a compass, a little book, a top, a baby doll inside a plastic case, could be anything. When I opened the prize, I got a little book with a picture of a sailor standing on top of the world. The caption said something to the effect of *"You Will Travel the World."* I was curious and didn't know what it meant, but felt it was a sign of things to come...

CHAPTER 2

My high school years were very sheltered. I attended Hauppauge High School from seventh to twelfth grade and graduated in 1970. During those six years, I stayed close to my family and the few friends that I had. I studied, did my homework, polished my bicycle, then my car, and watched the evening news, *Batman,* and all the other family shows that were on at the time with my parents every night. I especially liked *I Dream of Jeanie* because I had a huge crush on Barbara Eden. Let's face it, what teenage boy didn't?

I was afraid of girls. Based on my Catholic upbringing, I thought I could only have sex if I got married. I had been jerking off for years and was ashamed of myself for committing such a mortal sin over and over again. I actually believed I could never take it back or be forgiven. Based on that, I "tugged on my noodle" even more. I figured that if I was going to hell anyway, what was the difference, regardless of how many times I did it. I had *Playboy* magazines hidden under my mattress. When I got the urge, I would just grab one, look at the centerfold and let it rip! God, what a relief!

The magazines were in the middle of the mattress and I never knew if my mother saw them or not when she made the bed. If she did, she never said a word. Maybe she was embarrassed or afraid she would embarrass me?

In the summer of 1967, I got my learner's permit. My friend Will, who I met in eighth grade science class, was a little older than me and had a regular license. He had turned sixteen that July and I was going to be sixteen the following November. I had a learner's permit, but I was only allowed to drive as long as he was in the car with me. We'd go out to Montauk Point or the Hamptons for no other reason than to say we went there. It was a 100-mile drive, but gas was only 24 cents a gallon and we could fill up the tank for $3. Now, its $3 a gallon!

I had a brand-new 1967 white Mustang convertible that my parents bought for me with the stipulation that I make the car payments. They got it in advance of me turning sixteen because it was such a good deal that my father couldn't pass it up. It had a 289-cubic-inch engine, red leather interior, black top, folding back window, spoke wheels, 3-speed automatic transmission, and an AM/FM radio.

After we got the car, my father parked it in the garage and we just looked at it and polished it every day. We moved it in and out of the driveway, and then took it up and down the block. Finally my dad said Will could drive it as long as we were careful and didn't go too far away. When we went on our road trips, we cut school while my mother and father were at work. We always made it back before anyone got home. I loved that car and wish I still had it today.

Right after I got the car, I worked at Bedell's Sunoco gas station pumping gas and cleaning car windshields so I could make the $65 monthly car payment. Frank Bedell owned the place. He was a tough, hardheaded Irishman, but he was a good mechanic.

I was the cleanest gas station attendant that you ever saw! I would iron my pants and shirt and would always shine my shoes. The female customers always came to my side of the pump so I could wait on them. I made $1.15 an hour and pretty good tips.

One day, when I was doing something under the lift, Bedell had to go out to the pump and wait on a car. Driving it was a hot-looking lady named Joan, who happened to live on my block. Bedell was immediately smitten by her and they started a torrid and sultry affair. Eventually, his wife found out about it, as did her husband. Joan and Frank took off and were never heard from again. Years later, I heard that they left the state and got married.

Frank's ex-wife made out OK because they had to sell the station and split the money, but Joan's ex-husband was left with three kids and had a nervous breakdown over the whole mess. It was a big scandal in the neighborhood.

Sometimes in the summer of 1969, my friend Joel and I would take my car out to Robert Moses State Park, going over the newly built bridge on the Robert Moses Causeway to Fire Island. When we'd get to the bridge, we'd see girls with their thumbs out standing there in bikinis, hitching a ride to go over. We'd pick them up and give them a ride over the bridge so they could get to the beach. We tried to get them to stay with us so we could look at their boobs, but as soon as we got over the bridge past the tollbooth, they jumped out. They wanted no part of us horn dogs. They knew exactly what we were after and we weren't getting it from them!

In the fall of that year, my friend Will and I got a job at one of the first Baskin-Robbins ice cream stores in the country. It was owned by a lady named Mrs. Sipp, who was a real pain in the ass. We had to weigh every scoop of ice cream we served and every cherry had to be accounted for.

When she wasn't at the store, usually at night, we would give our friends free ice cream and make ourselves oversized sundaes loaded with every topping in the store. We would also listen to music from the bar next door. I remember hearing "Hey Jude" playing on the jukebox until we closed the store at ten PM.

Mrs. Sipp had a daughter named Ann, and Will used to bang

her in the back of the store while I watched the front. One night we accidentally left the freezer doors open and, in the morning, thousands of dollars' worth of ice cream was a melted mess on the floor. We both got fired and Willy ended his relationship with Ann. The mother hated both of us for melting her ice cream and she even accused us of stealing money from her. We never did, but another guy named Pete, who worked there, was the thief and he blamed us.

In the winter of 1969, the airwaves were filled with many songs that I'll never forget, like "Build Me up Buttercup," "Hooked on a Feeling," and the Temptations and their unmistakable Motown sound.

Earlier that year, I fell in love with a girl in my class named Doreen. I literally followed her around wherever she went. I was obsessed with her. She was a little taller than I was, blonde, and very pretty. There was something about her that I just liked.

That spring, I got enough nerve to ask Doreen to go out with me on a date and she said yes! The summer of 1969 was a special and a pivotal point in my life. Not only did we put a man on the moon, but I was beginning to understand what it meant to feel real love, at least that is what I thought.

During that summer, Doreen and I went on many memorable dates in my 1967 Mustang. I would work all week detailing cars and then get ready for my Saturday night date with Doreen. After a week of cleaning other people's cars, I would spend all day Saturday detailing mine so it would be perfect when I picked her up. We went to beautiful dinner venues all over Long Island and I even took her to the Jones Beach Marine Theater to see *South Pacific* with Guy Lombardo's Band of Royal Canadians.

Lombardo would zoom up in his beautiful, wooden Chris-Craft powerboat and step onto the stage to welcome everyone to the outdoor amphitheater for the show. I will never forget how the volcano erupted over the water near the edge of the stage for one of the scenes in the show. It spewed smoke, fire, and lava. It even sounded like a real volcano! Amazing...

That summer was magical and I remember looking at Doreen with puppy—dog eyes and kissing her sweetly on the cheek every time I dropped her off from our dates. I was in love with her in the purest way. I especially remember turning on the radio and listening to "My Cherie Amour" by Stevie Wonder, the biggest hit of the summer, and "Sugar, Sugar" by the Archies. As the summer turned into fall, I continued to date Doreen, never getting any closer than kissing her on the cheek.

Christmas 1969 found me leaving my parents' house on Christmas Eve and going over to spend time at Doreen's house with her family. She lived with her three sisters and her mother. Her father had passed away from a sudden heart attack two years earlier. Her sisters adored me and her mother especially liked the way I was respectful to Doreen, opening car doors, buying her flowers, and always complimenting her on how she looked.

1970 was the year that we graduated from high school. In January, the school put on a production of *The Sound of Music*. Doreen got the teenage daughter's role as Liesl von Trapp and I became the stage manager for the production. I got to see Doreen rehearse every day. On opening night, I got her a beautiful bouquet of roses. The winter was fast turning into spring and the senior night talent contest and prom were coming up, with graduation to follow in June.

Unbeknownst to Doreen, I had written a song about her for senior talent night, and I got up on stage and played it in front of the whole school. Doreen was mortified and ran out of the auditorium and all the way home. I had totally embarrassed her and she didn't come to school for three days.

Two days later, I went over to her house, apologized, and asked her to go to the senior prom with me. First, she said no, but then her mother convinced her to say yes. So in early June, I took Doreen to the senior prom.

On prom day, I sent one hundred assorted colored daisies to her house and, because she was taller than me, I purchased with two weeks' pay Adler's elevated shoes, which made me two inches taller. I rented a canary-yellow tuxedo.

As I look back, I must admit it looked pretty cheesy. When I went to her house, her mother and sisters greeted me at the door and showed me into the living room. As I waited for Doreen to come down the stairs, I also had in my pocket a charm bracelet for her that said, "I will wait forever," which was the first line of the song I wrote for her.

When Doreen came down the stairs, she was in a beautiful dress, but her hair was in a beehive hairdo and she had on high heels. Even with my elevated shoes, she was now a good six inches taller than me. As we departed for the prom, her neighbors and family started taking pictures of us and, because of our height difference, they made me stand on a milk box! I was totally humiliated!

When we arrived at the prom, everyone was staring at us and, when we started to dance, our height difference was obvious. My head was buried in her breast and as the Classics Four sang "Stormy," the night wore on.

After the prom, my parents threw a party for everyone at my house. A good number of people showed up for the free drinks and food. Doreen was with me, but she also was paying attention to several other guys, including one in particular who had graduated the year before and was with his own date for the prom from our graduating class.

About four AM, everyone went home and the other guy offered to drop Doreen home on his way back to his house. She accepted and said goodnight to me and left my house. I didn't know what to think, but

I did know that the next night, I was taking Doreen to the Rainbow Room in Manhattan to see Frank Sinatra.

At four PM that Saturday, I pulled up in Doreen's driveway, knocked on the door and she quickly came out in another party dress, but this time without any fanfare. She seemed tired, but I felt she knew that I had made these arrangements well in advance so she probably felt obligated to go with me.

Because I was still only seventeen when we graduated, I didn't have my full license that enabled me to drive outside of Suffolk County and into the city. I took the chance anyway and there we were, going through the Queens Midtown Tunnel, on a Saturday night in New York City traffic. Somehow I managed to get us to the NBC building and parked. It was a short walk to the elevators that took us up to the Rainbow Room. When we got to the restaurant and showroom, I bribed the maître d' with forty dollars and he set our table right next to the showroom floor. I smiled, knowing Frank Sinatra would be singing right in front of us and that was exactly what he did.

When the dinner came out, we were at a cocktail table so small it could barely fit our plates. We ate and then the lights dimmed and Ol' Blue Eyes himself came out with the spotlight on him. As he made his way around the room, the spotlight was also shining on us. He sang all of his hits and, as his final song, he sang "Strangers in the Night" right to Doreen with the spotlight shining brightly on them both as the whole audience stood up in applause. Doreen was captivated by the moment and impressed by all the trouble I had gone through to make the night happen. I could tell, however, that the show was over, for her and for me. At this point, she was just being polite.

By this time, it was one AM and we were exhausted from being out late two nights in a row. It was time to make our way out of the city and back to Suffolk County. I could barely stay awake while driving home on the Long Island Expressway at that wee hour of the morning. I was also afraid if I got pulled over, I would be arrested for driving with a junior license.

We managed to make it home and I barely kissed her goodnight as she got out of the car. She told me not to bother walking her to the door. After I dropped her off, I went home and went to my room, took off my suit, and passed out on my bed. I was exhausted both physically and emotionally, but I knew it was fading with Doreen. The buildup to the prom and the night at the Rainbow Room was overwhelming, but was something that I will never forget.

After graduation and all the prom festivities, the summer of 1970 turned out to be interesting to say the least. Doreen was going to attend nursing school in Manhattan in August and was moving to the city.

It turned out, after speaking to a few of my friends who had graduated the year before, that Doreen had been dating Mike Stahl, the guy who came to the prom with another date. While I was buying her flowers, taking her to expensive dinners and writing songs about her, Mike was taking her to McDonalds, buying her a hamburger, and banging her in the back seat of his car!

On the advice of my friends, I staked out her house one Friday night when she declined to go on a date with me. I watched Mike come over and pick her up. They kissed passionately when she got into the car and then they took off. To top that, he had a beater, piece-of-crap station wagon that he took her out in, most likely so he could take her in the back, lay her down and whack her brains out. I was totally crushed about Doreen and because I wasn't going off to college like everyone else, I decided to get three jobs and forget about her.

CHAPTER 3

At this point, I wasn't sure what I was going to do, so I decided I would just try and make money and focus on my car, friends, and my motorcycles. For the next two years, my friend Will and I would work on our cars, hang out with Steve and Louie on Friday nights, and go to the Ground Round, drink whiskey sours, eat hamburgers, and throw peanuts on the floor. I worked during the day at Del Labs in Farmingdale, New York, as a lab technician, sampling the formulation for Sally Hansen "Hard as Nails." Del Labs was owned by Charles Revson, of Revlon. He would visit the factory every Friday, always saying hello to me as he walked in. My office was right in the front of the building and I could see his black Lincoln limousine pulling up when he made his weekly visits.

He would brag about his nephew, Peter Revson, the famous race car driver, and how well he was doing. When Peter was killed two years later in a racing accident, I heard from my contacts who still worked there that he never came back to the factory again. Mr. Revson died two years later, many said from a broken heart. His nephew was truly the apple of his eye.

In addition to working at Del Labs, I worked at Roy Rogers Roast Beef making sandwiches and mopping the floors until closing every night. On Saturdays, I worked at a florist in Hauppauge, delivering flowers. Every Sunday, my three closest friends would come over for dinner. My mother would cook a big Italian meal and my friends would bring pastries from Rigi's Bakery. The tradition of the Italian dinner at 1:00 PM every Sunday was always a staple in my life, which continues to this day.

The highlight of the next year was when I went to see Elvis Presley live at Madison Square Garden on June 6, 1972. I asked a girl named Cindy Kline, whom I knew from high school, to go with me as a friend. Only once, in the spring of 1970 did we get into the shower together. She looked at my penis and said, "I have no attraction to it, so we should only be friends." Another let down, but I said OK. That was that and besides, she was banging a guy named Richard who was tall and must have had a big pecker.

By 1972, Richard was gone and Cindy and I were still friends, so that night we took the Long Island Railroad into the city. As we approached Penn Station, the whole city was electrified by Elvis performing at the Garden. Everyone was going to the same place and it felt like a religious experience.

I was eight rows away from him and I was mesmerized when he took the stage. As the flashbulbs went off, the crowd erupted and I could barely keep my eyes open. He couldn't sing for over twenty minutes until things calmed down. Elvis kept walking back and forth on the stage, holding his cape up as the audience continued to go wild. Yes, he was that good and you had to be there to believe it!

To this day, I've never seen any performer like him and I'm glad that I am one of the few who had the opportunity to see him live. I remember the highlights of the show being "Unchained Melody," "Blue Hawaii," "Jailhouse Rock," "Suspicious Minds" and an excellent rendition of Neil Diamond's "Sweet Caroline." This remains one of the stellar events of my life.

Two and a half years had gone by since graduation and I felt I was at a low point in my life. My friends had all moved on to college or had just moved away. I was still living with my mother and father, and during that time, I had had over thirty jobs, doing everything from landscaping to working at Macy's, selling shoes and hats. I had never had sex. Almost 20 years old and still choking the chicken, and still thought I was going to hell for doing this. The Italian guilt thing again! It's in our DNA; we can't shake it no matter how hard we try.

While I was working at a men's clothing store, I met a Puerto Rican girl, Rachel. On our first date, she wanted to have sex. I was so excited and scared I didn't know what to do, so I brought her to my house and into my bedroom when my mother was at work. Rachel immediately took all her clothes off and I couldn't stop staring at her large breasts. I was so excited that I grabbed both of her tits at the same time and came prematurely on her chest. She then smacked the shit out of me and said, "Take it easy, little fella."

Shortly after that, she inserted my penis into her pussy and it felt wet and sloppy. When I told her I couldn't feel the walls of her vagina, she laughed out loud and said, "That's because it's been stretched out by a lot of well-hung, much bigger guys than you. And your cock, Honey, I hate to tell you, is pretty small."

I remember being horrified and totally embarrassed! My first sexual experience and it was a real letdown. It made me reluctant to have sex with any woman ever again! And the guilt was overwhelming, so much so, that I was even ashamed to go to confession. I tried to bring myself to go, but just couldn't.

Other than having sex for the first time, which was a terrible experience, this was the real low point in my life. All I did was work, come home, and do it all over again. I felt like a rat on a treadmill. On top of everything, I was going on 21 years old.

On the advice of my father, I looked into joining the Navy. I drove down to the recruiter in Smithtown and I took the aptitude test. They said I was smart and I would qualify to go to Class A School for meteorology. I signed on the dotted line and in early 1973 I left for boot camp in Great Lakes, Illinois.

Oh shit! What did I do now, and what was I in for next?

CHAPTER 4

I will never forget the cold, rainy morning when the recruiter's van pulled up in front of my house at five AM. I said goodbye to my parents and my dog Buttons, and headed to off to Fort Hamilton in Brooklyn for processing before boot camp. As soon as I got into the van, I wanted to turn around and go back to my house, but it was too late.

The ride to Fort Hamilton was depressing. There were eight recruits, most of them black, in the van and nobody said a word for the two-hour ride there. All I kept saying to myself was that I had ruined my life and I wanted to go home.

When we arrived at Fort Hamilton, I had to be inducted, which meant the officers told me to take off my clothes and they looked up my ass while all the big, naked black guys stood in line, watching. The black dudes all had bigger cocks than mine and I remember feeling very inadequate…again.

After the exam and processing, we all got trucked over to LaGuardia Airport and took off to Chicago to go to boot camp in Great Lakes, Illinois. When we got to the airport, we boarded the plane and all the new recruits acted like we were going on vacation. They had never been out of the ghetto, and they were hitting on the flight attendants and drinking heavily. I just kept to myself and stayed quiet for the duration of the trip.

Once we landed in O'Hare, the party was over. The company

commander from the Navy was there with a list of our names and we were told to shut up and follow instructions. A few of the recruits, however, continued to talk and joke around. Their bad behavior was short-lived; the company commander belted one of them in the mouth and we all watched him bleed. At that moment, we all knew we were in the Navy and in boot camp. That was that! What a reality check!

The next nine weeks were terrible—the tear gas chamber, freezing cold, the room filled with fire and the strange mixture of people. We would wake up at four AM to a blaring loudspeaker, get dressed in three minutes, and then march in the freezing cold for two hours before breakfast. I was in shock, but they did not give us much time to think about anything except surviving.

They targeted one recruit in particular. While he was sleeping, several recruits poured warm water on his wrist and to my amazement; it caused him to pee straight up in the air. He woke up with the company commander and everyone else laughing at him. This got him a medical discharge after they found him and his bed full of piss with no reasonable explanation.

I can still remember the Company Commander entering our barracks each morning and his loud deep voice saying, "Drop your cocks and grab your socks, you maggots, and hit the grinder." My first night in boot camp I went into the bathroom, hid in a stall and cried profusely for my mother, keeping as quiet as I could.

Somehow I made it through boot camp and graduated in March of 1973. Everybody's parents came to the graduation except for mine, since they couldn't afford it. I was all alone on graduation day until one of my fellow recruits invited me to join his family for dinner after the ceremony.

The next day, Saturday, we all got leave and several of us got on the train to Kenosha, Wisconsin. Once the train pulled in, we noticed many cars lined up at the station. Carloads of female hookers, mostly black, were just waiting for the young, horny Navy newbies with pockets full of money that we couldn't wait to spend. It was obvious they did this every week as a new class graduated from boot camp.

One by one, we all jumped into their cars and off we went to these little, horrible apartments scattered all around the city. There were three or four of us in a room at a time, all having sex and then they'd take our money. When we were all done and had left the apartment, we had to beg strangers for cab fare in order to get back to the train and back onto the base. We came to learn that all the new sailors got taken like this on a weekly basis.

Upon my return to the base, I got orders to meteorology school in Lakehurst, New Jersey, which also meant that I got thirty days' leave and a plane ticket back to New York. I couldn't wait to get home!

Shortly after I landed in New York, I knew something had changed…perhaps it was me?

As I walked out of the gate, a few of my old friends were there to greet me. We caught up quickly and had some laughs on the car ride home.

When I arrived at my house, it all felt different. After hugging my parents and my dog, I headed into my bedroom and unpacked my duffle bag. As I sat there in silence, I was overcome with a sense of loneliness. I sat for a long time and then went back into the kitchen to have lunch with my friends and my mother and father. When we were through and everybody left, I went for a long walk in my neighborhood. It felt like a ghost town. Almost everyone I knew had moved off to college, or gone off to start their own lives. In just ten weeks away from home, I realized I had experienced a lot and it became apparent that everyone I knew had changed as well.

My thirty-day leave felt like an eternity. I was alone most of each day until the evening when my parents would return from work and my friends would then come pick me up so we could head back over to the Ground Round for a hamburger and more peanuts on the floor. After a few of these evenings, there wasn't much to talk about and I felt like a fish out of water.

When my thirty-day leave was over, it was the beginning of May and I was off to service school in Lakehurst, New Jersey. It was a four-hour Sunday drive, and the short distance from home felt good until I arrived at the base and checked into the barracks. Almost immediately, I knew I wasn't free anymore. I was assigned to be a Fire Watch, which meant I had to look in everyone's room and count the bodies every evening into the early morning. By the time my shift was over, I was only able to get two hours of sleep and having a crazy roommate didn't help.

My roommate was named Fred and he was always beating his meat. I got tired of hearing the bed squeak as he tugged on his noodle. When he came, he would scream and then it got quiet. What a roommate to have...

Every morning we'd be up at five AM for roll call. We'd march, eat, and go to class where we stayed for the next eight hours.

Two female recruits were in the group. The "WAVEs," as they were known, had their own barracks with other female Army, Navy, and Marine recruits. In my school, there were two women to every seventy male recruits along with twenty male Marines.

Women in the armed forces were still a relatively new concept at that time and I remember how all of the male recruits, including myself, wanted to bang them. One especially attractive WAVE, Sally, sat right next to me in class and I could tell we were going to be something.

When we initially started hanging out, we would get together every evening after class, but we'd go our separate ways on weekends. I went home to Long Island and she'd go to her parents' place in Wilmington, Delaware. This routine lasted for a short while until we each started living separately near the base. This led to us spending weekends together at Seaside Heights, New Jersey. During the summer of '73, our relationship moved from innocent friendship to animal attraction, which was solidified when we finally had sex in the front seat of my 1972 Dodge Dart at a graveyard in New Jersey.

It was a humid, hot, and steamy summer night. We ripped each other's clothes off and I used a rubber. After we were finished, as I pulled it off my cock, suction caused the rubber to fly across the dashboard of my car and hit the windshield, oozing cum all over. It was a sticky, dripping mess, but we were now a couple.

Soon after, everyone on the base knew we were an item. We would sneak off on breaks and have sex under the stairwell every day. I would lift up her skirt and give it to her while she held her panties to the side. It was exciting, very sensual, and only took a few minutes, a "quickie," and on the Navy base to boot! This made it extra hot…

We became inseparable, and weekends meant going to her family's house in Delaware or to mine in Long Island. My parents thought she was just okay, but they were not ecstatic about me being in a relationship. They felt I was too young to be getting serious with someone.

As the New Jersey summer dragged on, we both knew we'd be separated by the end of service school unless we did something like get married. So we did just that in the fall of 1973, got married on a Saturday that September in Wilmington, Delaware. Her parents were against it, as were mine, but we both insisted and had a small, hastily put-together wedding with friends and family at the church where her parents attended services every Sunday. After the ceremony, the weekend passed and we went back to the base to begin life as a newly married couple in the Navy.

To my surprise, the Navy was very accommodating and they stationed us together out at the Naval Post-Graduate School in Monterey,

CA. At the time, we were only one of a handful of married couples in the Navy and initially it seemed like the ideal situation.

We drove across the country, stopping at the Grand Canyon, hiking down from the South Rim to the Colorado River and back. That took all day and we finally came back up on the zigzagging, donkey trail, near death from the almost vertical climb back up the canyon wall. There was no shower in the little cabin we rented, so we had to take a bath in an old fashioned, standalone bathtub with only lukewarm water. In the morning our bodies were so sore that we could barely get back into the car.

We eventually got to California in the fall of 1973 and got an apartment on Sloat Avenue, right across the street from the Navy Post-Graduate School. The Navy assigned us the same duty section, so our schedules would be the same and we would never be apart. At the onset, married life in the service was pretty good, at least for a while.

For the next few years on the Monterey Peninsula, married life consisted of a routine of us going to work on the base, coming home, and socializing with three other Navy couples. On weekends, we'd occasionally go to parties or travel to San Francisco. Things were going along okay until late in the summer of 1975. Then came a turn of events that was a sign of things to come. My penis became my worst enemy and as they say, the small head was making all of my decisions, most of them bad...very bad!

CHAPTER 5

My wife Sally had a girlfriend named Terry who needed a ride to San Diego. She was a WAVE in the Navy also. That's what female sailors were called. Terry knew I was going there for a three-day weekend to visit my friend Louie, a childhood friend from Long Island. She asked me if I could give her a ride there and since I was heading in that direction anyway, I said, "Sure, why not? I would be happy to."

The next day, Terry and I were on the road and I was aroused from the moment she stepped into my car. Terry was from the South, had a Southern drawl, a deep raspy voice, a pretty face and an amazingly curvy body. In addition, she had the librarian look with her glasses on and hair in a bun, which I thought was very sexy. She also had beautiful feet and toes and I was always a toe man.

As we drove, conversation flowed smoothly and I felt there was a mutual attraction between us. We had been driving for about three hours when we hit very bad weather just above Los Angeles on the 101. We were forced to stay over in a hotel for the night.

There was only one room left with only one bed. We were so tired from driving through the storm that we decided to take the room, thinking we would just crash. At some point in the middle of the night, I found myself holding her, smelling her perfume and sucking on her soft, beautiful, sensitive breasts. Touching them made her put her hands over her head and grab the pillowcase. She was tearing at the headboard and then biting her fingers. Terry had perfect boobs that I caressed and massaged, while she moaned as we rolled around in the bed. I had a full erection and somewhere in the excitement, I pulled off her panties and fucked the bejesus out of her. My dick fit perfectly inside her pussy and she was very, very wet. She cranked her legs up in the air and I pounded her like I was drilling for oil. I could see the sweat glistening on her forehead in the dim light and feel her body quivering all over, even after we were done. After about an hour of wild sex, she and I both came together and it was unbelievable. This was the first time I had cheated on my new wife and, oddly enough, I found it delightful. Terry was also married and this made the whole event that much more exciting.

When morning broke, we resumed our drive to San Diego. Shortly into our drive, Terry told me she felt guilty and that she would have to confess to her friend, my wife, or she wouldn't be able to face her again. I was shocked and speechless. After what seemed like an eternity of silence, I repeatedly asked her not to confess, but there was no changing her mind.

Once we reached San Diego, I dropped Terry off at her friend's house and I went to my friend's house for a three-day visit. When Terry got out of the car, I knew I wouldn't be driving her back and my life suddenly felt upside down.

When I got to my friend's house, I was shaking as I walked up to his door. Once inside, I immediately called my wife to let her know we had arrived safely, but she didn't answer. I knew Terry must have gotten to her first and had told her everything. I felt isolated in silence and guilt, with racing thoughts of what awaited me when I got back home.

It was a long, lonely drive back and when I walked into our apartment, I found my wife's father Paul sitting there with a lawyer. Paul said my wife, his daughter, was divorcing me and that it was over. I stood there frozen as he and the attorney left the apartment. I managed to walk into the bedroom where I lay down thinking for several hours before finally falling asleep. It was a restless night to say the least.

When I returned to the base in the morning, I learned that my wife had already gone to the brass and exposed me and the whole situation as it had unfolded. I was totally disgraced and embarrassed. Within a few days, the Commanding Officer had changed our duty sections so we would rarely see each other. I worked nights when she worked days. This was only until we could make other living arrangements or get our own separate apartments.

When the smoke cleared, I learned from the guys on the base, they had seen Terry and Sally holding hands while walking and also observed them stealing a kiss with each other. Wow, can you imagine this development? There I was getting divorced and the laughingstock of the base. It turned out that Terry was divorcing her husband as well.

Months later I ran into my ex with Terry and she was kind (or mean) enough to reveal that the car ride with Terry to San Diego was a setup that they both had planned. My ex- confessed that she had been in love with Terry all along and they had been together for quite some time. When I asked how long this had been going on, she said all of her trips to the store on the base were really chances to visit Terry. At that moment, I realized I had unknowingly married a bisexual, who in the end left me to be with her true love. As Frank Sinatra said, "That's Life." It sounds funny now, but at the time, I was devastated to think I was being played by the both of them all along and had no idea…

CHAPTER 6

After the divorce, I found myself alone when I wasn't on duty. For the next eight months of 1975, I lived in an apartment alone, returning home to a TV for background noise and a solitary lifestyle. I was depressed and living in complete boredom.

Then in early 1976, I got a roommate named Tom Burns. He was a cool guy but had a lazy eye so you never knew if he was looking directly at you or not. Shortly after he moved in, I learned Tom was a bit wild and liked to throw parties in the place every night after we'd return home from our work shifts. I could not deal with Tom's lifestyle and he was driving me crazy with the loud music and drinking. My living situation had gone from bad to worse and I began to avoid going home, often opting to go to Mission Ranch in Carmel Valley on the nights I didn't have to work.

One night, something life-altering happened. I met Anna, a beautiful dark-haired German girl from Heidelberg. I was drawn to her dark brown eyes and by the way she moved on the dance floor. She was seductive without even trying. So, I decided to come out of my introverted foxhole and get into the hunt.

I approached her like a sniper when she went for a drink at the bar. Slowly and methodically, I moved in and out of her line of sight. My liquid courage was flowing and as I got close, I waited patiently until she took a few sips of her drink. The next thing I knew we were in a conversation and she told me that she owned a massage parlor in a little town not far from Monterey. I probed further and she said she worked in Marina, which was right off the Main Gate of Fort Ord, the big Army base that is now closed. Without her saying as much, it became clear to me that she was a madam or a hooker. I was sexually deprived and lonely, so we started a friendship and romance.

When I wasn't working on the base, I was working with her as the host at the front desk of her massage parlor. I was all dressed up in a suit greeting servicemen as they came in for the various services that were offered. Before long, I knew all the massage girls who worked there and we all became friends. The girls knew I was the madam's man, so they kept it very businesslike. When Anna wasn't entertaining her "special" clients, she would take me into one of the little dark rooms in the parlor and she would suck and fuck the shit out of me. She would turn the heat up in the room, light candles, and strip slowly. It drove me nuts!

After we were through, we would go to Mortimer's, which was a cheap diner serving big-plate, greasy food. After a few months of this, I decided that we should live together and Anna was on board with the idea. At the time, she lived in Salinas, twenty-five miles away from the base.

As I packed up my car and drove to her mobile home, it dawned on me that I clearly wasn't doing much better with my monk-like, solitary existence, so what the hell, why not? I was twenty-three years old. What else do you do when you are twenty-three? Constantly getting laid was high on the priority list and I had a perfect setup—at least that was what I thought.

After I moved there, I quickly realized how difficult it was to drive back and forth to the base when I was on duty, especially in the morning after I had been up all night. When I was with her, we had threesomes with her friends and there is no doubt that being with two women is better than one. We played all the time and I loved her German accent. It was very erotic to hear her talking to me while I was fucking her. The foursomes were something, a real turn-on. Anna would invite a couple over and then we would all sleep in the same bed. As soon as the lights went out, she was grabbing the other guy's dick and his girlfriend was groping for me. It was so exciting seeing the other guy banging Anna while his girlfriend and I talked to them. Then we would start playing and she would guide her guy's dick into Anna's pussy. After that, she would suck on me and ask me to give her a good hard fucking.

She was skinnier than Anna, so she could really get her legs up in the air and wide open. Her box was shaved and during that time, a shaved pussy was quite unique. It was smooth, wet, and tight, plus she was a real screamer. The more we watched Anna and the other guy, the more turned on we got and harder we fucked. At one point, we all came together and it was one hell of a rush! Then we would all get up and have breakfast.

After they left, Anna would ask me to describe what I saw and how I felt while it was going on. Then we would get turned on again and I would give it to her another three or four times. She was always ready and a ferociously exciting lover.

I felt I was getting more and more into sex. It became an addiction that would never let me go. The more I did it, the more I wanted it! Anna taught me everything she knew and I was a good student and she was a great teacher! She taught me how to find a woman's G-spot with my tongue and not many men knew about this. She would actually give me lessons and instruct me as to where to place my tongue, how to manipulate it and then how to go up into the vaginal canal and hit the spot.

This skill served me well for the rest of my life and kept every woman I got involved with hanging on, at least for a little longer, because of the value-added service they were receiving from me.

One day, or night I should say, we had a problem. I fucked Anna twelve times that day and had to work the "midwatch" night shift that evening from seven PM until seven AM the next morning. I took a short nap before going to the base, but I was so tired I could barely stay awake.

When I got to the base, I almost fell asleep at my desk twice. As the night wore on about eleven PM, an OP IMMD came in from a nuclear submarine in the task force. An OP IMMD was a rapid response request from the fleet for data, based on an immediate exercise or wartime operational need. It was my job to input the latitude and longitude into the primitive computer with punch cards and get the readout from the computer, then send it back to the submarine.

Because I was so tired, I accidentally typed the latitude and longitude into the punch cards backwards and when the data came out and I sent it back to the sub, it went the wrong way as in turning away from the task force and going in the opposite direction! Oh, shit...oops!

The next morning my relief came in and I handed over the night watch details to him. At this point no one other than the admiral and commanders in the task force knew what had happened. I was fucked and didn't know it yet, so I went home and went to sleep. About an hour later the phone rang and it was the Lt. Commander. He said, "Lazano, get your ass in here ASAP. We, or you, have a major problem and wear your whites!"

I tried to ask him what was wrong and he said, "Don't ask. Just get in here."

I said, "Yes, sir."

When I got back to the command, there were no smiles or hellos. I was told what I had done and they considered it a dereliction of duty and I was most likely going to be court-martialed! Now what? A perfect Navy record and, because of marathon fucking, my record would be trashed!

As the day for the preliminary court martial came closer, I learned that two full captains would be determining my fate. I was getting more and more nervous. I knew I could be actually busted in rank or possibly go to the brig. Either way, my military record would be destroyed—all because of fucking. The day before the hearing, I spoke to my immediate supervisor, Lt. Tom Wortham. He told me, "John, just tell them the truth."

I said, "Really?"

He said, "Yes."

I went home that night and didn't sleep a wink. In the morning, I was in the hearing room at 0700 hours, waiting for all the officers and captains to arrive. They all started coming in and not one of them looked at me or spoke a word. They lined the walls of the room on each side and I had a military JAG officer as my Navy-assigned attorney. Then the two captains came in.

Everyone stood at attention and then they sat down. The captains took their seats at the front table, looking back at everyone. It was quite a scene. At this point they led me out in the hallway, and then they summoned me in. I walked in at attention in my whites and walked right up to them. They had all the documents relating to the incident, including messages from the submarine that went the wrong way based on my bogus information. I thought I was doomed for sure and would go to jail for sure. Then the big moment came…they read the charges against me and I just stood there numb.

Then one captain, the one from the *Iowa,* asked me to explain exactly what had happened that day and night that would result in this mistake on my part. You could hear a pin drop in the room. Everyone was holding their breath waiting for my answer. I remembered what my Lt. told me, "Tell the truth."

I looked straight ahead and paused, then said out loud, "Captain, sir, I had sex so many times that day, I was exhausted and disorientated. I came so many times I was weakened and could barely remember my name…Captain; I basically fucked myself into a coma…"

There was a very long pause…everyone was in shock and speechless, but I could see they were trying not to explode with laughter. The captain looked shocked as well. He began to get red in the face and he looked up and down and at the other captain and paused, then said looking down, "Dismissed…don't let it happen again!"

I said "Yes, sir," then turned around and marched out of the room. All the officers came out single file behind me and went to a nearby hallway and fell on the floor laughing! They were actually crying and couldn't believe I had said what I said. Lt. Wrotham came up to me and said, "See, I told you to just tell the truth," and that's exactly what I did.

Shocking as it was, the truth set me free! I only got a letter of reprimand put in my file and that was the end of it. I was returned to full duty.

Even after all these years, this story is still told and has become legendary on the base.

CHAPTER 7

After the court-martial, I felt stronger than ever about Anna and felt that I loved her. After all, we had sex three times a day on average and she always swallowed my loads. Why wouldn't I love her, are you kidding? Remember, she was a prostitute and that was her job. How could I hold that against her? I didn't know anything about a woman's body until I met her and she showed me the ropes. Long before the G-spot was discussed, she showed me where it was.

I decided that I was going to bring Anna home to New York to meet my family. Once this happened, she would become a good girl because she was in love with me. Yeah, sure, what a dummy I was!

Before I brought her home, my father asked me what she did for a living. I told him she was a hooker and the phone went silent. He said, "Oh my God, are you freaking crazy? You will give your mother a heart attack!"

I said, "Dad, I love her."

He said, "You only love what she does to your cock!"

Wow, was he right! Anyway, can you imagine a traditional New York Roman Catholic family meeting their son's fiancée, a full-blown German hooker with serious road miles on her face? By the way, she was twelve years older than me to boot!

So the day came, and we flew from SF to JFK on a 747. During the flight, I whacked her in the bathroom and became an official member of the famous Mile High Club.

I went in first and she came in behind me, then she pulled up her skirt, moved her panties to the side, and sat on my cock. She was dripping wet and gushed all over me. She moved up and down and side to side until I came. I exploded inside her and it only took 2 minutes, but it was so exciting to think that we were fucking on the plane! We cleaned up as well as we could, then left the bathroom about two minutes apart and went back to our seats.

What a rush! We even had some turbulence while we were screwing. This made it extra special!

When we landed at JFK, my father picked us up and I only remember him looking in the rear-view mirror...and he did not say a word. He was just looking. Years later he told me that he wanted to bang her, also...so there ya go. I always thought he was a little jealous and as it turned out, he was. Anyway, when we got to the house, my mother was so upset that she took to her bed and said that she was going to die.

When I went to my mom's bedroom with Anna, she saw that my mom was sick. Anna told me to get out of the room and my mother and her spoke for a while alone. Anna told my mother that she loved me, but that I was just a baby to her and that she would be kind to me. Anna made my mother soup and they held hands, but that night Anna and I decided to stay in a hotel because it was just too intense to stay in my house.

The next day, I asked her to get married, and she said, "Why not?"

We drove out to Riverhead, Long Island, got a marriage license, and got married by a justice of the peace in the courthouse. We got a tree trimmer out of a tree and a cleaning lady to be our witnesses. After we got married, on the way back to my house, we pulled over and Anna sucked and fucked me in the car as a wedding gift. I gave her a wooden ring that I bought for five bucks…crazy!

But it's all true! I married a hooker and after we made love in the car, as we approached my house, she decided the whole thing was a mistake. I had to take her directly to the airport and get her a flight out of Newark back to Monterey, CA. That was it, she was gone! We had only been married for four hours!

When I finally got back home, I was rattled and told my parents the whole story. My father wanted me to see a shrink and my mother wanted to take me to see a priest. The next day, we got a lawyer and went to get the marriage annulled. My mother had to stand up in court and tell the judge that we had never consummated the marriage. She did it because that's what Italian mothers will do for their sons…

Twelve days later, I flew back to Monterey and headed directly over to the massage parlor. Anna was there fucking away, drinking, and making money. I walked in and told her we were done and she said, "Great," and then she proceeded to fuck the shit out of me. It was the best sex ever!

After that, I got my stuff out of her trailer and moved back to Monterey. I missed Anna, but I mostly missed the wild, hot, deep fucking, sucking, and the delicious pussy licking with Anna screaming and moaning. At least Anna taught me what a woman likes and where to find it. To this day, many men do not know and I've realized that being great at sex has its disadvantages in that there's always a price to pay for something so pleasurable. My life has been haunted in a way, leaving my mark on many women along the way. But I must say that they all seemed to go nuts when I got my tongue into their pussy.

While in Monterey, I dated a famous Hollywood actress. I will not tell you who she was, but I met her in a bar when her first big movie came out.

I met her when we were both in Carmel Valley at the Carmel Valley Ranch Country Club. I didn't know who she was, but I was captivated by her as I was standing around the piano singing with all the guys in the Navy. She was sitting under dim light at the corner of the bar when she said, "What does a girl from Wales have to do to get attention around here?"

I immediately approached her. I had no idea who she was. I introduced myself and said, "Hi, I'm John," and she said, "Hi, I'm Ashley."

I said, "What do you do?"

She said, "I work for a legal firm." It was bullshit, but what did I know? We sat there at the bar talking until two in the morning when she said she couldn't drive, so I decided to drive her in the pea soup fog to wherever she had to go.

In Carmel, fog often rolls in during the middle of the night and this night was no exception. Once we got into my car, she told me she was staying at a guest house somewhere down in Carmel Valley. I found out later it was actor Efrem Zimbalist Jr.'s guest house.

I somehow got us there and we wound up falling asleep in her bed. By then, it was too late to drive back to Monterey and the fog was too thick. It was a small house behind a main house, so I had no idea where I was.

In the morning, we woke up and whacked each other's brains out in a love affair that lasted for over a year. I finally learned who she was and every two weeks she'd come back to Monterey. In those days, there were no cell phones or social media. It was a much slower time and if you wanted to, you could disappear and get laid secretly...it was easy.

As the affair progressed, she asked me to fly to LA to meet her. I'll never forget when she came to pick me up with her Jackie O sunglasses on. She arrived in a 1968 Cadillac, top down, with her hair back in a bun. I got into her car and she took me to Benedict Canyon Drive or wherever the hell she lived and this whole thing was like a dream come true.

As the relationship continued, it became obvious to me that I was her boy-toy. She took me to some Hollywood parties where I met some A-list stars. It was clear I had to keep sexually performing for her because it was my job—that was the only reason I was there. Once we were in bed, as soon as my tongue got near her beautiful, plump vagina, she would explode in an eruption of pussy juice, swearing and screaming out of control, while telling me how much she loved it in her British accent. I barely touched her and she went ballistic. I guess Anna taught me well!

This went on for about four more months when I was finally faced with the decision to either get out of the Navy or re-enlist. In spite of the incident with the submarine and based on my appearance in my whites, I became the poster boy for the Navy and was selected by Command to be the attaché to the admiral for the Sixth Fleet in Gaeta, Italy. This was a dream come true. I accepted the orders and prepared to re-up. The actress was climbing the ladder of success and it was no secret that we were going in different directions.

On March 14, 1977, I was all set to reenlist and go to my new post in Italy. My new orders were in hand and waiting to be executed. I was going to be the Admiral's right-hand man and go with him to Geneva, wake him up, carry his briefcase, and make sure his uniform was dry-cleaned.

Little did I know that my father had called Command and told them that my mother was dying and that I had not been home in over two years. He said I had disregarded his pleas to come home and visit my mother. This was all bullshit, of course, but it was his way of trying to get me not to go to Italy for six years…and it worked. After the phone call, I was summoned to the administrative office of the admiral and the captain told me that I was a bad example of a family person because the Navy was big on family. They immediately gave me thirty days leave and ordered me to go home, deal with my family and help take care of my mother.

The window for the Italy assignment was only a week and I either had to go or I would lose the orders. Because I was ordered home, they would not hold the orders open for me and I was screwed. I lost the assignment and had to be discharged. I was devastated. I only had enough money to take a Greyhound bus across the country back to New York.

After a five-day trip, the bus pulled into the Port Authority Bus Terminal on Eighth Avenue and there were my parents waiting to take me home, to take me away from the grip of the devil and save me from myself, or at least that is what they thought....

Now I was a civilian, back in the room that I grew up in. I found myself with no money, no pussy, no actress, no Italy. I became very depressed and I called the actress daily from a pay phone, burning through a ten-dollar roll of quarters each time. After a while, she must have disconnected her number because it didn't work anymore. It was over and I was back in Long Island on unemployment, drinking, hanging out in smoke-filled bars and "jerkin my gherkin" every night alone.

CHAPTER 8

It was now April of 1977, and I was trying to get a job and finally did. I was making $150 a week at a factory, so I was going to work, going home, and going to the Ground Round two nights a week to eat hamburgers, step on peanuts, and drink screwdrivers. As sweet and horrible as they were, I would down at least six of them a night.

I met a waitress there and we decided to go out and whack each other all night. This was strictly lust. She said she was horny and needed it, and I told her the same. After she got off work, we headed down to the beach and did it in the car, right in the parking lot. When we came home in the morning, the cops were in my driveway and my mother and father were crying. My father starting screaming, "Where were you?"

I said, "I was out getting laid! Is that all right with you? I'm a man of twenty-four years old who has been out on his own for over four years."

The cops were laughing their asses off. I was so embarrassed, but I had to set my parents straight. They, however, had other ideas that included getting me hooked up with a good family girl with a similar background.

In May of 1977, disco was the rage—actually it was the beginning of all of it. I did not wear a polyester suit well. I hung out with my friends and all we did was ride around in circles, go into NYC, eat, get drunk, and try and get into Studio 54. We polished our cars and never hung out with any girls. One Saturday, my parents came home and said they had fixed me up on a blind date with a lady's daughter they knew from Charles and Sons, a dime store in Commack Corners, a local shopping center at the intersection of Jericho Turnpike and Commack Road.

My mother and this lady got their hair done together and decided that we would make a good couple. Her daughter Kristen had just gotten home after a bad marriage in upstate New York and needed to meet a nice guy. My mother gave her the phone number to our house—no cell phones in those days—and she was going to call me that afternoon. I was pissed, but I must admit I was curious to see what she looked like.

She called and introduced herself. We spoke for a while, and then made a date for the following evening. I didn't know what to talk about, after my crazy life in the Navy and all the things I had done, but made polite conversation nevertheless.

She came over to my house and I made her a cup of coffee and accidentally set the dishrag on fire from the gas range. I put the fire out and we had the coffee as we sat on my front steps while I played the guitar for her. She seemed to like me right away and I liked her because, in all honesty, I was very lonely and so was she.

We went out on two dates and after the second date she wanted to go to a motel and have sex, so we did. It was OK, nothing that I was used to, but it was better than nothing. She thought it was great! Let's face it, after Anna and everything else I had done, I was a well-trained, professional sex machine who had learned from the best! A person like me was very new and exciting to Kristen and for that matter, would be to any normal, conservative woman brought up on Long Island in the 1960s and '70s.

At this time, I was working at a florist shop on Saturdays and in a factory during the week—I always had at least two jobs. Kristen worked at a bank five days a week, getting off every day at four o'clock. It became routine and mundane. Every Saturday when I'd get off from work at the florist shop, we would go out to dinner. After dinner we'd go to a motel and stay out all night. The next day, Sunday, we'd go to my mother's house at one PM for the Italian family dinner.

This went on throughout the summer and, while I liked the companionship, I wasn't quite sure whether or not Kristen was the one for me. She was five-and-a-half years older than me and had gone through a terrible marriage that ended in divorce with her first husband. I never got the whole story but in any event, we continued to go out as 1977 dragged on.

August 16, 1977, was the day that Elvis Presley died. The factory where I worked only had a radio and a bulletin came on at three PM Eastern Standard Time, announcing that Elvis Presley had been taken to Baptist Memorial Hospital. Another bulletin came on at approximately three-thirty with the shocking news that Elvis was dead.

When everyone left work, people were rolling their windows down, spreading the news while women were crying. I remember cars almost crashing because people were so preoccupied and disturbed by his death. When I got home, I turned on the TV and all that was on was nonstop coverage at Graceland.

That night President Jimmy Carter addressed the nation, saying that a great tragedy had occurred with the loss of one of the greatest icons in music history, Elvis Presley. The country literally mourned for days as we watched Elvis's funeral unfold on TV in surreal footage of white limousines, his viewing at Graceland by all the celebrities, then the final funeral procession. It was riveting and I was glued to the TV for the entire thing. I even took time off from work to watch it. His popularity was worldwide and his talent very much underrated. There will never be another Elvis Presley. I was glad I got to see him in person.

During this time, Kristen and I continued to go out and, as the autumn of 1977 set in, it became clear that we were in fact going to be a couple. My friend Will had been going out with Patty, and my friend Steve was going out with his neighbor, Tricia. We all began to go out together on triple dates, and every Sunday we ate at my mother and father's house as part of the Italian dinner ritual. My friend Louis also came except he didn't have anybody and he was alone most of the time.

Patty and Willy were engaged and they were set to get married in September 1977. I was his best man and Kristen went with me to his wedding. Steve worked at Ralph Oldsmobile in Smithtown as a mechanic and Tricia worked as a nurse in the local hospital. Everyone seemed relatively happy although I must say after the life I had led in California, this new routine seemed very boring and it wasn't what I wanted.

I resigned myself that this was the way it was going to be for life as a married couple on Long Island in the late 1970s. This included the dinners and family gatherings on holidays, with everyone sticking relatively close together.

A few weeks before Thanksgiving of that year, my friend Steve came to our house on Sunday as usual, but he was coughing. It was an odd cough and it would not go away. This went on for days. After the second week my father said to him, "Steve, when you go to the doctor, get an X-ray. It sounds like you might have pneumonia."

Steve took his advice and that following Tuesday the X-ray revealed that he had a gigantic tumor wrapped around his heart that was considered inoperable. That fateful afternoon he came back from the doctor with a death sentence. One day he and Tricia were a couple planning on getting married, the next day he was told that if he lived for six months, he'd be lucky. Needless to say, his family, Tricia's family, and all of us were devastated. His mother, sister, and father freaked out. That first day, everyone was out of control and we all assembled at Steve's house in the evening to try to talk some sense into everyone and come up with a plan as at that moment there wasn't any. My father even came over.

We all discussed it and suggested that Steve go to Sloan-Kettering Hospital in New York and have them evaluate him. He did and they said that while the tumor was inoperable, they thought they could scrape most of it off his coronary arteries and eventually get the rest with radiation. It was a long shot, but they gave him a 50/50 chance to live through the operation. These odds weren't good enough for his family and they declined this course of treatment.

Back in the '70s, very little was known about this type of cancer and how to deal with it. Steve's main doctor was at Huntington Hospital in Long Island and their level of expertise was limited at best. They suggested radiation…this consisted of cobalt treatments that were radical and draining, but they thought because he was young, he would be able to tolerate it and the tumor might possibly shrink. Steve declined this and with every passing day you could see that he was getting worse and worse.

Someone in his family consulted a nutritional doctor who said he should fly to Haiti to pick up boxes of various fruits and herbs and then blend them together to make a drink that would help poison the cancer out of his body. He and his family scraped the money together to go there, purchase all the stuff, and then come back. He began to drink these drinks on a daily basis and he got skinnier and skinnier, declaring that he felt great all this time.

By the end of January 1978, his ankles began to swell and two weeks after that he was in Huntington Hospital unable to walk. Throughout February and March 1978, we visited Steve on a daily basis, which gradually turned into every other day as hope began to fade. Near the end, I was the only one who visited him on a daily basis and watched his decline with each passing minute. By the end of March, it was clear he didn't have much time left. The doctors weren't sure if he would last a month, two months, or six months. They just didn't know.

It's funny because when I went back to his house one of those days, his mother asked me to look at his closet and take a suit out. The suit I selected had been my suit. He and I were the same size and we even wore the same size shoe.

Steve passed away in April 1978. He died right in front of me at six o'clock in the evening while his mother was feeding him. I'd never seen anything like that before and I must say it affected me for the rest of my life. His mother and one of his sisters went crazy in the hospital—screaming and crying and insisting that he be revived—but it was to no avail. He was gone.

His uncle had bought him a brand-new black 1978 Toyota Celica that was parked in the parking lot of the hospital, visible from Steve's window. Steve never got to drive the car. It was only there for him to look at.

While everybody expected him to pass away, it was still a shock. Because Steve's family were strict Catholics, he was to be laid out for three days at the local funeral parlor right on Commack Road. My father and I were the very first ones into the room at two o'clock that day for the viewing. Steve had a full open casket and he was wearing my suit and my shoes. He looked like he was sleeping. He had his glasses on and was wearing his high school ring. He actually looked pretty good considering he was so skinny when he died.

Right then and there, when I saw Steve in the coffin with my clothing on, something shot through me like a bolt of lightning! I remember thinking to myself, *Is this it? It all ends in a box and then what happens?* While I believed in Christ and the afterlife in heaven, I was absolutely struck by the idea that Steve's life had been taken from him at twenty-six!

Something inside me told me at that moment that I should live every day like it was my last and take every chance that I wanted to, because you don't get a second shot at it. This revelation because of Steve's death set the course that I would take over the next thirty-five years.

I'm not sure if it was good or bad. I only knew a light went off inside of me that told me to do anything I wanted to do and have no regrets because, at the end of the day, when the lights go out, they go out and you only get one round! The image of Steven in the coffin has never left me to this day and I have carried his Mass card in my wallet ever since.

During the three days of the funeral, which the whole town attended, these thoughts were at the forefront of my mind. The day they laid him to rest in Pine Lawn Cemetery was rainy, cloudy, and cold, and all I remember is them lowering the casket into the ground and saying goodbye to the man who had been my best friend. It even makes me cry now to think about it.

After the funeral and burial, we went back to Steve's house and had the traditional food that the family prepares after a wake. Steve's mother and sister were inconsolable and his father didn't say a word. The pain was evident on all their faces and all of the faces of Steve's relatives. Steve was a good kid. He never smoked, never drank, never did drugs and always worked. He loved his mother and his family and was a very dutiful son. Why God did this to him was always a question I asked myself and still do.

After Steve died, nothing was the same. Willy, Patty, Kristen, and I went out, but Tricia never came again. She was devastated and never recovered until middle age. She finally married in her late thirties—over fifteen years after Steve's passing.

CHAPTER 9

As the summer of 1978 began, Kristen and I began to do things on our own. Willy and Patty had gotten married in September 1977, and they lived relatively far away. Will was pursuing his career, getting a master's in finance from Hofstra University. Patty was working as a legal assistant and they didn't have as much time as they used to.

I remember in late July 1978 going to see *Saturday Night Fever* when it first came out. I knew then that Kristen and I had been a couple for quite a while, but I still wasn't sure if she was the right one for me. One day in late July 1978, she was lying on her chaise lounge in her mother's backyard. I told her that I didn't want to see her anymore and I went home. She was crying and didn't understand why, but I just knew deep down that she probably wasn't the right one for me.

I went home and told my father and he said "Good," because he didn't think she was right for me either.

After that, I tried to go out with several girls I had met while out in those days. There was no such thing as online dating or cell phones. I met a few girls and I went to have a drink every time they gave me their phone number. It never worked. It seemed like everybody was hooked up with somebody by the time they were twenty-five years old.

I found myself going to work, coming home, being alone, and not having a direction. After all, I had been through the Navy and after all my adventures there, this seemed to be a dead end. I kept reflecting on what my father did to me when he deprived me of the orders that I had to be the assistant to the admiral in Italy. My whole life would've been different, but at this point that was old news.

After one month of being alone, I decided that I would make a go of it with Kristen and I called her house to see if I could get together with her. Her mother said she had gone to Las Vegas to visit her aunt and she gave me the telephone number where I could call her. I hesitated a couple of days, and then I called.

I asked her how she was. She said okay and she missed me. I'm not sure what possessed me, but I asked her if she wanted to get married when she came back, and she said yes.

Right after that I wasn't quite sure what I had done, but I knew I had asked her to get married. This time I had to try to make it work. After everything I had been through, I did not want to go through it again. In Long Island in the late '70s when you got married, you got married for life. Upon her return, we set a wedding date of September 11, 1978, and we got married in her mother's living room by a justice of the peace. Our parents, her brother, my sister, and no one else sat down at her mother's dining room and had dinner after the very limited ceremony.

At that time I had just gotten a job as a regional sales manager for a flow meter company in Long Island. I was making $18,000 a year and I qualified for something called the Farmers Home Mortgage. With that I purchased our first home in Long Island. One month after Kristen and I got married, we moved into this little ranch house with the railroad tracks behind it.

Kristen had a dog named Heidi and she came along with us. I drove to work about twenty miles west on the Long Island Expressway and Kristen immediately quit her job to go help her mother take care of her grandmother, who was dying in Huntington Hospital, the same hospital that Steve had been in.

With my job as a regional sales manager, I began to travel extensively. I was in charge of all the representatives in the southeastern United States, all the way to Texas. I had never traveled until I took that position and I'll never forget my first trip.

Kristen and her mother took me to LaGuardia Airport on a Sunday afternoon. I had to fly to Texas to meet our rep and travel around Texas to do a trade show. I was a bit excited, but I wasn't excited to leave home because I knew once I was free, my old habits and feelings would creep up on me. I longed for the excitement of a new challenge and a new tight little pussy to get my hot dick into.

The first five seconds is the best! The new feeling of a new woman, with all the hot new moves that go along with it—what a thrill! Whether they know it or not, most men run for this, they will do almost anything. It's the hunter in all men.

As soon as I was on the plane, I felt a new feeling of being free. I started to flirt with women, hiding my wedding ring and eventually putting it in my pocket. When I landed in Texas and was picked up by Frank Miles, our rep, I could already see the party was going to get started that evening. I was at a Holiday Inn and in those days that's where all the action was.

Frank dropped me off at the hotel and told me he'd be back at seven-thirty the next morning to pick me up. As soon as I went into the bar, many women began looking at me and flirting—talking to me and telling me how handsome I was, something my wife never did. I felt like I was back in the Navy again and the fact that I had married Kristen never entered the picture. I felt that I was away from home and whatever happened, happened, especially after remembering Steve lying in the coffin. I didn't care what I did.

That evening, I met a gorgeous blonde who was traveling and staying in the same hotel. We hooked up that night and, in the morning, parted ways and everything seemed just fine. For whatever reason, I had no more Italian guilt. It was gone.

When I traveled, I was on the road for a whole week at a time, going to bars and staying in hotels every night with a whole group of guys. Everybody was married, but nobody seemed to care. Since, there were so many beautiful women in every town we traveled to, this was a bad habit to get into, but we did. At the end of the week on Friday, we all began to fly out to go home and all went through a metamorphic change, back to reality.

When I landed back at LaGuardia, Kristen came to pick me up and, of course, I told her what a difficult week it had been and how hard I had worked. From then on, everything was a little strange on the home front. We had sex, but nothing like it had been in the beginning. It slowed to once a week, then to twice a month. That became once a month, then not for months at a time...

With my traveling schedule, I was always getting ready to leave and Kristen was always busy dealing with her sick grandmother. That became a full-time job for her until her grandmother finally passed away.

About that time, I received an offer to be the national sales manager of a competitive flow meter company in New Jersey. I drove over to New Jersey, got the interview, and they hired me. I became responsible for all United States and European sales in a job that required me to travel even more than I did before.

The guys I worked with were all crazy about going to strip bars and chasing women. As a matter of fact, my first and only interview was in a strip bar with the vice president of this company. I had to drink and take lap dances in order for them to hire me, and I did.

During the week, I had to stay in the Sheridan in Woodbridge, New Jersey. I left our home in Long Island on a Sunday night and drove to New Jersey, went to the hotel and started work Monday morning. I stayed in the hotel Monday, Tuesday, Wednesday, and Thursday night. Friday afternoon, I left at about two and drove all the way back to Long Island through the terrible traffic. This went on for about six months. Then, after work, I began looking for homes in southern New Jersey so Kristen could eventually move there.

I started working with a realtor from Century 21 in Freehold NJ. She assigned me another realtor who was pretty hot to show me various properties in Jackson, a small town twenty miles south of Freehold and forty-five miles from my office in Edison. When I first met her, she came to the hotel and I introduced myself. After a couple of drinks, I asked her if she would like to go up to my room, so I could give her my employment verification papers. She said, "Of course, I need those anyway." She also said she would do anything for the commission.

As soon as we got in my room, she got on her knees and pulled my zipper down, then she unbuttoned my pants as she stroked on my cock, which was still in my underwear. In a soft voice she said, "Let's see what's in here?" In one move, she pulled my underwear down and had my cock in her mouth. She sucked me hard and fast and was looking right back up into my eyes. Then she stopped and pulled her dress off over her head, took her panties off and said, "I really need that commission." She proceeded to stand up, make my cock hard with her hands, and then put it right between her legs. She jumped up on the dresser and made me give it to her right there, on the edge of the dresser. Something told me this was how she made most of her "commission." I bought the house and during this time, going back and forth to look at the house, we continued to have sex several times a week. When I finally closed on the house and Kristen moved to New Jersey, my relationship with the realtor was over.

After a couple of months in the house, Kristen was pregnant with our first son, one of the few times we had sex. Sergio was born in Freehold Hospital in February 1981.

In the summer of 1981, it turned out the company in New Jersey was being sold and I was going to be out of work. My rep in Chicago, Mickey, offered me a sales position and I drove out to Chicago in September 1981 to start my new job. Kristen stayed in New Jersey with Sergio. Her mother came from Long Island to be with her, until it was time for her to move to Chicago.

I stayed in a room in my rep's secretary's house. Her name was Louise. Every evening her husband Paul would drink a fifth of vodka and fall out of his chair and on the floor. Louise was an older, attractive woman, who was incredibly horny. One night she snuck into her daughter's bedroom where I was staying, jumped on top of me and fucked the crap out of me. It was insane.

Every night, Mickey and I were out drinking, chasing women, and going crazy. Every happy hour, we ate dinner and then washed it down with drinks. I didn't have to go home, just back to Louise's house where she was waiting to suck my dick as soon as I walked through the door.

Louise was always in a negligee and she was always hungry for sex. She would moan, scream, and sweat while I fucked her and she would always say, "Give me more and don't stop." Her husband was passed out and it's clear that she was sexually deprived and could not wait to get her hands on me, or for that matter, any man that would give her some attention.

In November 1981, I purchased a home in Bolingbrook, Illinois, and Kristen was coming out with our son Sergio who was only eight months old. The night before they were to arrive, Mickey and I were in downtown Chicago and I had a hooker in the backseat of his car who was giving me a blowjob while he drove.

Without me knowing it, she took $800 from my wallet and the next thing you know, I didn't have any money left to buy the washer and dryer that I needed for the house. Kristen was due to arrive that next afternoon. In the morning, I had to borrow $800 from Mickey and a couple of the other guys I knew so I could buy the washer and dryer, then go to the airport to pick up Kristen and my new son. That was bad and I was out of control! I guess that the idea of needing to settle down once my family showed up was preying on me. I knew I had to stop all of this craziness, but could I? I wasn't sure...

CHAPTER 10

All of a sudden, my family was there. I had a hard time realizing that I couldn't drink anymore or stay out that late. I tried to stay home initially, but then gradually I stayed out later and later, typically leaving at seven in the morning and not getting home until nine or ten at night, usually drunk. It wasn't good.

In 1982, Kristen became pregnant with Chet, who was born in December in Naperville, Illinois. Several nights before he was born, I had been with several women and on one particular night, we were all at the Rusty Pelican drinking and I decided to go home. It was cold and snowing and I only remember getting behind the wheel of the car and then waking up in my driveway. I have no other recollection of driving the car, but I woke up stone cold sober in my driveway. At that moment, I realized I had to quit drinking, which I did and I also realized I had to leave Mickey and get a new job if I had any hope of curbing my ways.

I did all of that and for the next three years was a homebody. The new company I worked for let me work out of my house and we went to church every Sunday with our neighbors, the Dukes. We went on vacations, had dinners together, and lived in a very wholesome manner. Because both of our families were far away, we became each other's family and spent most holidays together. That was the calmest time in my life. We essentially spent every weekend with Eddie and Darlene and their two girls, Melony and Megan.

They were the same age as our kids, so it all worked out very well. We even made the Dukes godparents to our son Chet. They were wonderful people who set an example of what a family should be. Eddie and Darlene were the most gracious people you could ever want to meet.

In the summer of 1985, we all went on a memorable vacation. All of us left Chicago in my 1985 Chevy station wagon and went to Holland, Michigan, Mackinac Island, Sault Ste. Marie, Toronto, and Niagara Falls, then back. This was the best vacation I'd ever taken in my life. 1985, '86, and '87 were great. We even watched the 1986 Super Bowl together when the Chicago Bears won! Remember "Refrigerator Perry" and "The Super Bowl Shuffle"?

In the summer of 1987, I lost my job and sought a new position in Florida. Actually, an executive recruiter called me. Kristen's parents were living in Florida and mine were soon to move there, so it seemed like going to Florida was the right thing to do to be near both our parents. I got the job and the house in Bolingbrook went up for sale.

The day we left was a very sad one with the Dukes sitting on their front stoop with their kids and the moving truck in front of our house. At the end of the day, we left in our station wagon with everyone crying. We left the best friends anyone could ever have had.

On the way to Florida, I couldn't help thinking about how badly I had behaved in Chicago. As we were driving through the seven states, all I could do was think back about all the sex I had had while I was there. I had been with countless hookers, married women, waitresses, and God knows who else during the six years we lived there.

When I broke the news to Darlene that we were moving, she became physically ill and took to her bed. I still believe it was because she was secretly in love with me. I had told her about some of my adventures in the Navy, but never elaborated. She found it exciting and I could tell she wanted to hear more, but I never told her. Her husband was very nice, but a little boring and she led a sheltered life also, but I never crossed the line with her and never would have.

As we traveled to Florida, I was trying to promise myself that when we got there I would curb my ways. I was starting my new job at the Williamson Instrument Company as the national sales manager. I had two kids and a new house and I thought this change of scenery and climate would change how I thought about things.

When we arrived in Florida, we had to stay in a hotel for two days while the moving truck caught up with us. We now lived in Mulberry, Florida, a small town outside of Lakeland in the community called Imperial Lakes. We had a corner lot and a built-in pool and everything seemed like it was going to be just fine. Every time my penis got hard when I looked at another woman, I hit it with a ball-peen hammer to try to kill it. I thought it was working, but within one week of arriving there and beginning my new job, I realized that was not what was going to happen.

CHAPTER 11

When I walked into the new company on my first day, I was introduced to everyone, including the graphic artist, a girl from Peru named Maria. She was dark-haired, beautiful, and had a mysterious accent that I just loved. She had beautiful toenails and a very hot body. Needless to say I was smitten with her and here we go again…

Every morning when I got to the office, I would always say hello to her and look at what she was wearing. She wore very attractive outfits and open-toed sandals and that drove me insane! Many times when she sat at her drafting table, I could look up her dress and I could see her underwear. I was mostly interested in what was behind the underwear—her pussy. I could tell it was big and wide and needed to be filled.

I became friendly with her and she even met my wife and my kids. She was living on the other side of Lakeland with a much older man named Mario, a hotheaded Italian, who was very volatile. They had a tempestuous relationship which revolved around hot sex after they would have a fight. They were both thick-headed and played off each other's temper.

As I got to know her, she began to tell me just how much she hated the situation she was in. She had been divorced, came to this country, did not know much English, and was trying to teach herself to be a mechanical drafter. Wilkerson gave her a chance and she turned out to be a real talent, who designed circuits and did all the catalogs and brochures for the company. She was self-taught, smart and industrious, and hot as a firecracker, and that South American accent! Wow! I admired her very much, and that admiration served as a real aphrodisiac for me.

This friendly, businesslike association went on for about a year. Then one evening, I was working late at the company and so was she. I was about to go home, walked into her office to say good night, and suddenly I just couldn't help myself, and I kissed her. Then I grabbed her breast, pushed her bra down and started sucking it right then and there. We both knew we had something for each other, but she also knew I was married with two little kids. At first, she told me to stop and I did, but then she said, don't, just keep touching and kissing me.

As the days went on, we always managed to sneak off someplace after work to have a drink, make out, and touch each other. One day we both left work early and went to a hotel and had wild passionate sex. At this point I was sure I was in love with her. Oh my God, here we go again!

One day she did not come to work and it turned out she had been with a realtor and bought the house right next door to me. Can you imagine, right next door and she was going to move in two weeks!

She got my wife involved, helping her look for furniture and getting her set up. Initially she was eating dinner with us and we were helping with her house. I would help cut her grass and fix whatever was wrong whenever she asked me to. We both knew how wrong this was, but it added to the excitement when we were alone.

As it turned out, every time I went over there with my toolbox, she would end up sucking on my cock and then she would bend over and look out the window to see if my wife was coming across the lawn while I fucked the hell out of her the back way, then gave it to her hard and fast. I always had to tell her to be quiet. She would moan and groan and tell me, while I slowly went in and out of her, that, "The tip was bigger than the trunk." She said my dick was shaped like a "mushroom." Every time I put it in, she would squeal with delight and her eyes would roll back in her head. Then she started talking in Spanish. I don't know what the hell she was saying, but it sounded sexy. It made me blow my load over and over again. And she took every drop of it.

Then we started an advertising company where we would drive down to Port Charlotte, Florida, every Saturday and sell advertising space in a little magazine that we created for all the hotels. This was just an excuse to stop along the way and make love. We left at six in the morning and didn't get home till nine at night.

My parents had moved to Port Charlotte, and we always went to visit them when we were there. Now that I think about it, Kristen put up with a lot, but I was sure that I loved Maria and I didn't have any feelings for Kristen. Every time I approached her about our relationship, she always pushed me off. I felt confused, but I also never neglected my responsibilities to the children and Kristen.

After three and a half years in Florida, Maria decided she would move to Las Vegas to follow Mario, who was now living there. One day, Maria said I had to choose her or my family, otherwise she was leaving. I chose my family and she left.

I was devastated and missed her immensely. She was my best friend, lover, and confidant, and I relied on her for everything. Kristen suspected that we had an affair going on, but she never said anything. She only knew that when Maria left, I was in tears. She did actually ask me if I wanted to go with her, but I said no, I had to stay with her and the kids, and I did.

Suddenly in 1989, Jim Williamson fired me. He knew I was screwing around and he was also screwing around with his secretary and didn't like the idea that Maria had been with me. He figured she left the company because of me and he resented me for it. Now I had another opportunity to straighten things out at home.

In the fall of 1989, we moved to Dallas and I became the national sales manager for a Williamson competitor. Moving to Dallas turned out to be the worst thing I ever did. We got there and the apartment was small, the weather was terrible, and my new boss turned out to be a bastard. After only two months there, I told Kristen to go back to Florida with the kids, this time to Fort Lauderdale where her mother lived, and move in with her. On a cold and rainy day, she and the children got in the car and drove all the way back to Florida without me. I stayed in the apartment we had and my life got miserable after that.

My boss in Dallas made me travel all the time. I think he was trying to make me quit. I knew Maria was in Las Vegas and was working at the Flamingo Hotel. I called the Flamingo and got in touch with her and told her I was in Dallas and I missed her very much. She said she missed me, also, and loved me, so she quit her job, left Mario, and drove to Dallas. She arrived and we got an apartment together and now I was living a double life.

My nerves were always on edge because I was afraid my boss would get wind of it and would fire me. Maria got a job in a graphics company and we lived together for about nine months. Kristen got a job at the Police Department in Plantation, Florida, and her mother watched the kids. Because the company I worked for was half Japanese-owned, the people of Japan found out that my family had left me and gone back to Florida. They intervened and made my boss transfer me to Florida and open up an office near the apartment that my family had just moved into. They basically ordered me to go back.

I left Maria and drove back to Florida with my father, who had flown in to accompany me on the ride back. I talked to him the whole way back and we really bonded, but then I dropped him off in Port Charlotte and I went on to Fort Lauderdale and met back up with Kristen and the kids, while Maria continued to work at the graphics company in Dallas. The next thing I knew, she got a job in Tampa, Florida, and moved from Dallas to Tampa, just to be near me. I can say that she must have loved me, or she never would've gone to that much trouble. When she moved to Tampa, I made an excuse up to drive there so I could be with her.

As soon as I saw her I had to pull her pants down to her knees; I liked to see them halfway down. I gave it to her like a ravenous animal. She was so horny and full of desire that I couldn't believe it! She was Latin, and they are all like that once you get them going. Her pussy was wet and juicy and her nipples were big and hard, plus she knew how to suck on my cock just right. She would get on her knees and ask permission to let her "taste it." What do you think I said?

Now that she lived in Tampa, I would go back and forth every two weeks, just so I could see her. In between times, when I was home, I used to go to a Denny's on University Drive in Plantation where I met a waitress named Lucia, who was also Latin. She was another hot number. All she wanted to do was make me lick her and have sex. She got off work at two o'clock and she and I would go to a park near a little office that I had and I would finger her outside in the grass. She would scream in Spanish (I loved it), then make me take her in the little office I had and bang her on the floor, or the desk.

After several months the Japanese company decided to let me go. Sales were not doing too well and the boss in Dallas wanted to get rid of me. This was because he could not keep an eye on me at all times and he was a control freak.

Now it was 1991 and I had no job and I was living with Kristen and the kids in an apartment on University Drive in Plantation, Florida. She was working at the police department and I was frantically looking for a job. I did not want to work in the industrial sales market anymore, so I started looking for other jobs and I ended up working for a dentist in

North Miami Beach. My job was to call on lawyers to talk about TMJ, a type of jaw disorder that many people would get from the impact of being in a car accident. Many dentists at that time were getting into treating this disorder because the insurance companies paid big bucks to them as part of the injury claim.

I was only being paid about $35,000 a year and this doctor was extremely difficult to work with. In Yiddish he was a true "meshuggena," crazy. He would throw things and go nuts when something didn't go his way. I couldn't work with him. Even though he was fifty-two, his mother was the only one that could calm him down. We had to call her many times to come to the office just to get him under control. Can you imagine a grown man and having to deal with all this? He was a real maniac!

A well-known plastic surgeon walked into the office to get his teeth cleaned. He looked at me and said, "What are you doing here?" I said I had just started working there two months ago.

He said he needed a guy like me to work in his practice and he wanted to have dinner with me the next night. That next evening, we met at Mark's Place on 123rd Street in North Miami. We talked and hit it off right away. He offered me the position as administrator of his practice making $85,000 a year. I accepted on the spot and said I would give my notice to the nutty dentist the next day. I couldn't wait to get out of there!

As soon as I got in the car, I went to a phone booth and I called Maria. I told her to move to Fort Lauderdale because I had gotten a good job and now we could be together. She left her job in Tampa and moved to Fort Lauderdale into a beautiful garden apartment that I got for us on Dania Beach Blvd. It had vaulted ceilings and overlooked the pool. It had every amenity you could possibly ask for. We even had our own washer and dryer right in the unit. It was a real love nest.

I left Kristen and the kids and moved in with Maria. At the time I served Kristen with divorce papers, but she never signed them and put them in the dresser drawer. Maria managed to get a job with an advertising firm in Miami Beach and began to do very well.

Maria and I and the plastic surgeon and his wife, or girlfriend, started to do things together and became very good friends. We would go to social functions and marketing meetings and I began to make the doctor famous on the Miami scene. South Beach was the big rage in 1992, and the doctor was fast becoming the talk of the town. We even hung out with Gianni Versace before he was killed. The doctor named the son he had with his girlfriend after him.

After Hurricane Andrew, we moved from a small office on 123rd Street to the Turnberry building in Adventurer, Florida. We set up an incredible office that is still there to this day. The doctor and the facility have been in magazines and publications all over the world for its exceptional design and his incredible talent as a plastic surgeon. In 1993, I got the doctor named best plastic surgeon in Miami. After the magazine came out, a line of women who wanted plastic surgery stretched out the door into the street. The practice went from $500,000 year to over $1.5 million in the course of the next six months. It was amazing!

One day a beautiful blonde named Corrine walked into the practice. The doctor was smitten by her and they went into the exam room for a long time. Even the nurses knew they were banging each other. The funny thing was that Corrine liked me also, and we began to see each other after work and on Saturdays when Maria was working.

Corrine and I would drive over to Naples, Florida, across Alligator Alley, have lunch in a nice restaurant on Route 41, get drunk, and get a hotel room for the rest of the day. We would suck and fuck and she made me put my pecker between her large breasts. Her thing was her giant tits. She loved to use them. While I fucked her, she would put both of her nipples in my mouth at the same time. Then she would say she couldn't breathe. She was an animal. We would make love at least five times in an afternoon.

I began to have sex with Corrine almost every day—after work, in the car, in the office, even outside. She was hot to trot, about six inches taller than me, with milky white skin and a gorgeous body. My pussy-licking skills came in handy with her. She would scream and cry every time I got my tongue on her G-spot. She would literally lose it! We even went on a vacation together to the Grand Canyon, Memorial Day weekend of 1992. Oh boy, what a trip that was!

After we returned, the doctor sat us both down. He fired me and hired her in my place. She took over everything I had built for over two years and resumed banging the doctor. I was devastated and out of money and luck. Maria found out that I had been with Corrine and she told me to leave. I went back to Kristen and the kids and began to look for a new job. This gave me another chance to reunite with my family, but as with all the other times, it failed. Luckily, Kristen had the job at the police department and I was able to get unemployment that kept us going until I found work.

One day I answered an ad for an environmental salesperson. I walked in and they hired me right on the spot. Mike, the vice president, asked me if I had any experience in the environmental field and I said no. He said, "Great! You're hired."

I started working at Permafix Environmental Services in Davie, Florida. At the time, it was called Integrated Resources Recovery. They made me a salesman and I literally knew nothing about the environmental field. During this time I buckled down, stayed close to my family and tried to live a quiet life again, but not for long…

CHAPTER 12

The opportunity for another wild relationship came up and I jumped at it. During this time it was clear that Kristen and I did not get along. She only tolerated me and I tried to get counseling, but she did not like the idea and blew it off. She told the counselor that she did not want to discuss her personal life with a stranger. At least I tried…

In 1994, while working for the environmental company, I decided that I liked environmental work and I went back to college to get a degree in environmental technology. I excelled at it and the company made me hazardous materials manager for the firm. About that time I began to talk to the cruise lines. Actually, I managed to secure a $2 million account by getting all of Carnival Corporation's business when it came to the removal of hazardous waste and oily bilge water from all of their vessels.

Even though I secured this business for Perma-Fix, I answered an ad to be a part-time salesman for a medical device company. When I arrived for the interview I was greeted by Sherri, the Regional Manager and we immediately hit it off. She was thin, very pretty, had an athletic body, brown hair and brilliant blue eyes. She also had beautiful feet and toes, always painted and always perfect. Her breasts were small, but she lit my candle with her beautiful smile and vivacious personality.

Man, did I have the hots for her, but she had a boyfriend she had been with for twenty years. When she saw that I was getting into the cruise industry, she started getting much closer. At the time, Sherri was living with her boyfriend, but one night he beat her up, threw her furniture and clothing out the window and then in a rage, threw her into the street. He was drinking and they got into a huge fight because he didn't like her hanging around with me. When all this happened she called me in a panic and even though it was ten o'clock at night, I ran out of the house and found her walking in the street several blocks away. I felt I had to rescue her because she literally had no place to go. That night I got her a hotel room and the next day I got her into a safe, guard-gated, apartment complex.

The first night she moved into the apartment, I brought Chinese food over because everything was a mess and she was trying to get organized. I came in with the food and she was just getting into the shower. She said she would be right out, but then she asked me to bring her a towel if I could find one. I walked into the bathroom where she was on her knees totally nude and dripping wet. She told me to come over to her so she could suck on me. We started kissing and before I knew it, we were all over the floor doing a 69, and then she let me kiss her hot little toes one at a time. She knew I liked her toes because she always caught me looking at them. She even wore a thin ankle bracelet that slid down onto her calf when her legs were open and up in the air. This gave me a great visual while I was doing her. She knew how sexy it looked, and we always did it with dim lights on and in the daylight, so I could see the whole thing as I looked from side to side.

After five weeks of staying in the apartment away from her boyfriend, she started up with him again. I went to the apartment one night and her car was missing. On a hunch, I decided to drive by Robbie's house, Sure enough, her car was parked in the driveway and all the lights were out. I called her, but she didn't answer and the next day she moved out into her own townhouse five miles away. It turned out her mother gave her money to purchase the townhouse, move, and buy furniture. Luckily, I was able to get out of the lease without it costing me a fortune, but I was upset because of everything she had put me through. Regardless, after a while I would go over to visit her and sometimes take her to dinner, but our visits were limited because Robbie was always coming over right after I left. Even if we did go to dinner, when I brought her home, he was right there in the parking lot waiting for me to leave, so he could stay the night. They just couldn't seem to stay away from each other no matter what. They had the typical yin-yang relationship. She always said she was breaking up with him, but never did.

In the summer of 1995, a Holland America ship, the *Westerdam,* was pulling into Fort Lauderdale. A key executive of the company came off the gangway and asked me—before he even got down to the dock—if I wanted to train all the people on the ship in environmental awareness. The light went off in my head and I decided to start my own company. At that point "The Hazardous Materials Specialists" was born!

I incorporated in the summer of 1995 and went on my first and last cruise with Kristen that August. She wanted to come with me, but was mad at me the whole time because I was working and did not have time to spend with her. I took my vacation time in order to take this cruise and was a total nervous wreck because I had never done anything like this before, and, if it was a failure, I risked losing my job. This first trip was a trial run and whatever the captain said was how Holland America would gauge if the training was something they wanted to continue or not.

When I was asked to do the training, I had never trained anyone in my life. I went home, took all of these comic books from environmental handbooks and cut-and-pasted them together into a makeshift training manual. Every crew member got one of these booklets and I created slides to go along with them. The cruise lines were paying me $35 per person and on my first cruise I trained over six hundred people. I made over $18,000 in one week.

In addition to the training, I invented a chemical drum system and a variety of other products that included developing a special machine that would grind up fluorescent light bulbs and safely extract the mercury from them and contain it. The cruise lines all purchased these products and found them useful in identifying chemical hazards while saving them money and helping them by providing them solutions to many of their daily, on-board environmental issues. The bulb machine was a big hit. At one point, every cruise line purchased a machine for every vessel in their fleet. Some are still in use today.

At the end of the cruise, the captain reported back to headquarters that the training was very valuable and they should sign me up for the rest of the fleet to train all crew members! I took two cash advances on MasterCard and quit my job. I even came up with a uniform that looked like I was in the Navy. It included white shoes and a captain's hat. I created special epaulettes that had three bars with a hazardous waste diamond in the middle. It looked great! People weren't sure what I was, but it all looked official and made everyone listen to me, plus all the women always gave me a second look.

I looked like Tom Cruise in *Top Gun*. I even wore the dark aviator sunglasses. My entire house turned into a training book printing facility and Kristen helped make copies of the books after work. Every time I went on a cruise, I would have to carry a thousand books with me. This was an unbelievable task, but the company took off like wildfire and we made over 50,000 training manuals in nine years. Within several months, all the cruise lines hired me and began sending me all over the world.

From that summer on, nothing would ever be the same again. The money flowed in like water and I literally traveled for over forty weeks a year. The women all loved the uniform and this got me in lots of trouble. Of course, Sherri knew what I was doing and since our breakup, I hadn't gotten a good job. I needed someone to go on the cruises with me to help me with all the presentations and she was the perfect choice. She had been a schoolteacher, and, in late 1995, Royal Caribbean, Celebrity, Norwegian, Cunard, and Carnival Cruise lines hired me to sail on all their vessels, on every itinerary, everywhere they went—all over the world!

I was overwhelmed and needed help. Much to the dismay of Robbie, I offered Sherri the job and she accepted without hesitation. I created a uniform for her and paid her $2500 a week. She sailed with me on the first twenty-two cruises and after that I moved out of the house and opened up an office in Port Everglades. At about that time, I purchased a 32-foot Avanti cruiser. It was a beautiful boat with a cuddy cabin and twin Mercury I/O's. With a little practice, I learned to navigate and maneuver it around like a pro. I kept it docked down by Shooters on the Intracoastal Waterway, where it turned out to be an incredible "chick magnet."

When I was at Shooters in my uniform, everyone would ask what I did. I told them about the cruises and, of course, they all wanted to go with me. The fact that I had a boat was icing on the cake. I got laid so many times on that boat, I lost count. Sherri was hanging on because she liked going on the boat and she loved the money she was making, but her boyfriend was putting pressure on her to leave the job and not go with me on any more cruises.

Again, I was in love with Sherri and she knew it. I spent every waking moment with her on all these cruises and we literally went from the Mediterranean to Singapore and all over the world together. One time, we flew to New York, stayed in the Plaza Hotel, had dinner at the Palm Court restaurant and went to see *Phantom of the Opera* at the Majestic Theater. The next morning, we set sail out of NYC on the *Queen Elizabeth*.

We sailed with Regis Philbin and his wife Joy, Swoosie Kurtz, and several other celebrities. Regis pulled up to the port at the same time we did, saw me in my uniform, and referred to me as "Commander." It was great! We crossed the Atlantic and attended all the captain's parties and formal nights. The cruise lines sent us everywhere: Singapore, Hong Kong, Le Havre, France, literally all over.

We made love everywhere, even on the front of one of the ships, just like in *Titanic*. Because she had small boobs, she made up for it by knowing how to suck me into a coma, and then swallow it slowly while she moaned. She would make me eat her while she spread her pussy wide open, showing me her glistening, wet clit. It made me insane and I got used to the fantastic blowjobs, eating sessions, and sex with her tight little body on all the cruises that we went on. Believe me; I could see why Robbie, her boyfriend, kept hanging on.

After all we had gone through she became a big part of my life. In early 1997 I asked her to get married, but she said no because she was still with Robbie. I was overwhelmed by the fact that she would go with me on a trip, then go back to Robbie, who would berate her, then he would make her have sex with him to prove she still loved him.

One time, I was just pulling into her condo complex to drop her off and he came out of her house, drunk, ripped her right out of the car and told me to get lost. As I drove away, I heard him tell her to get into the house and get ready because he was going to fuck her like the slut that she was!

In a strange way, I think she liked this kind of twisted game. It looked to me like she wanted to comply with his order; I think it turned her on. That got me sick, so sick that I called my cousin, who I had go to the office, meet Sherri and terminate her for me. I didn't have the balls to face her myself. She had a spell over me and I was like putty in her hands. I said yes to anything she wanted, I just couldn't help it, but now she was history.

Sherri was gone and I was doing the training all by myself. This was very difficult, but I was free from Sherri and all the stress of not being able to win her love. No matter how well I treated her, she could not get away from the dysfunctional relationship she had with Robbie. After that, I never saw or heard from her again. Although, I recently learned from Facebook that she and Robbie had moved out of state and stayed together for another 21 years—until he passed away. Apparently, in spite of everything, they were always in love and had an unbreakable bond. After all those years, I finally understood.

In March of 1997, I resumed my training schedule alone, but little did I know what was in store for me next...

CHAPTER 13

Kristen must have known that I was not faithful to her, but it didn't seem to bother her. The kids were growing up and she was working while I was going on my cruises. I was literally gone for forty weeks during calendar year 1996, and 1997 was shaping up to be a year of even more travel.

After Sherri was gone in January of 1997, I met an unbelievable number of women in a two-month period that I had brief sexual interludes with. These women were ambassadors' wives, dancers, social directors and many, many more. I sailed from Florida to Bermuda to the Bahamas, South America, Europe, and Asia. It was an unbelievable way to make a living and I literally couldn't believe the job that I had created for myself.

I had a secretary initially, named Cindy, who was a real bitch. I'm still not sure why I hired her. In early 1997, she brought her friend Judy into the office to help because we were getting busier and busier. Judy was heads and tails better than Cindy, and when Cindy and I got into a fight, I fired her and hired Judy full-time. She turned out to be the best assistant and administrative aide that anyone could ever have.

By March of 1997, it was me, Judy, and my son Sergio, running the Hazardous Materials Specialists. Not only did we do training, but we also did the hazardous waste removal from all the cruise ships coming in and out of Fort Lauderdale, Miami, Port Canaveral, and the Port of Tampa. The business grew to $1 million-plus a year and we were so busy that we all could barely keep up with it. Based on our boom in business, I decided to get a new, bigger boat.

I upgraded to a fifty-foot yacht! It had twin Cummins 330 diesel engines and an eight kilowatt Westerbeke generator. It had two full bedrooms and bathrooms. After I got it, I installed three flat-screen TVs. It was spectacular and I spared no expense in fitting it out with the latest and greatest of everything that money could buy!

In those days, the boat dealers faked everything to the bank and it was easy to get a larger loan. The new boat I purchased cost over $350,000 and the payment, after the trade on the old boat, increased by $1200 a month. What the hell, why not, I was making $50,000 a month-plus. It was a tax write-off.

I was afraid of the new, larger boat, so I hired a captain to show me how to drive it and signed up to go to sea school in Ft. Lauderdale to become a real captain. I became a captain and then a 100-ton master. I got into it and became very good at maneuvering this large vessel in and out of all the boat slips at all the restaurants up and down the Intracoastal Waterway from FLL to Miami.

Because I now was a Master, with a merchant marine license from the Coast Guard, this gave me further credibility with the Cruise Lines, and they gave me even more work! The new boat brought even greater visibility around FLL and I became known as "Captain John." I zoomed all over town in a beautiful new black SL 500 with the top down. All the valets knew me and they would always park my car right up front, so everyone knew when I was there. Down at the dock, I had my own reserved parking space.

During that time, I became somewhat of a local celebrity at all the hot spots along the Intracoastal Waterway and I loved it! The women came at me like bees swarming to honey and I literally could not keep them away. You might ask, could there be more? Yes, I'm afraid so…

CHAPTER 14

I sailed out of Miami in March 1997 on the Royal Caribbean ship *Legend of the Seas*. We headed out of the port into the south Atlantic to Curacao, a small Dutch island just north of South America. It took us twenty-four hours to get there and on that first night, the seas were rough.

That night was the "first night" formal party that turned out to be pretty uneventful. I attended the dinner in my dress whites and was a guest at the captain's table as usual. After dinner was through, I turned in early.

The next morning, we got into Curacao and I decided that I would get off the ship and take a taxi ride to see and learn a little about the capital, Willemstad.

I disembarked about nine-thirty AM and had a taxi take me all around the town. I paid the guy forty bucks and told him to show me all the spots and points of interest so I could learn more about the culture and the city. We drove around for a while and then I had him bring me back to the ship at about one PM. I decided I would get some sun and take a rest before I had to do my training the next morning. Originally it was scheduled for that day, but they changed it based on the cruise schedule, so I was essentially off for the rest of the day. It was a beautiful sunny day and I put my bathing suit on and headed out to lie on a chaise lounge on the deck and fell into a deep sleep.

The sound of a whistle in the distance woke me up. It actually startled me. At the same time I woke up, a girl who was lying next to me woke up at the same exact moment. We both sat up and looked at each other and another immediate lightning bolt attraction occurred. Our eyes were locked on each other and I asked her name. She said Tamara, from Minnesota. I said that my name was John and that I was from New York. She had already figured that out based on my accent.

We both started laughing at the fact that we woke up because of the whistle going off and then started a conversation that lasted over three hours. She was bubbly, smart, and extremely attractive. I immediately felt that I had known her all of my life. She seemed to like me and our conversation went on and on. We talked about everything I did on the ship and she told me all about her being a pharmacist for Walgreens and that she was on the cruise with her parents and her cousins for family vacation.

Because it was now five o'clock, everybody was going back to their cabin to get ready for dinner. Tamara invited me to her table to have dinner with her and meet her family. I accepted and headed back to my cabin to get ready. I was excited because this was the first time since the fallout from Sherri that I had met someone that I really liked.

When I arrived at the dining room, I immediately spotted her and went over to the table. I met her mother and father and a cousin and everybody seemed to accept me very graciously. When I explained what I did on the ship, they found it fascinating and found me even more interesting. Her father was a doctor and her mother was a high school principal. They were both very smart and affluent. Tamara had a seven-year-old son from a previous marriage and he was on the cruise as well.

Tamara looked beautiful in her cocktail dress, but all I kept looking at were her high cheekbones, beautiful eyes, and her vivacious smile. She was of Norwegian descent, smart, sassy, had a great sense of humor and I was falling for her as the dinner went on. Her son was pretty well behaved. The grandmother, Tamara's mother, kept him under control because she could see that Tamara and I were hitting it off.

After dessert, Tamara and I headed off to the Schooner lounge to have a drink and continue to get to know each other. It seemed like we had our own private party going on regardless of who was around. We sat in a booth, ordered a few drinks, and continued to talk about everything—our lives, what we did wrong, what we did right, and everything else.

While we sat there, I could tell I was falling for her. She seemed to have everything that I wanted in a partner and in a woman. I found her intellect the most attractive thing as I continued to get to know her and the fact that she was beautiful was icing on the cake.

During the evening, I'm not sure what time, all of a sudden, we just started to kiss each other passionately. We couldn't stop making out with each other. Her lips were soft, sweet, and very fulfilling. I felt her soul through her kisses. Just at that moment, her mother and her cousin came into the lounge and saw us making out. They immediately turned around and left.

Tamara and I really got into it and she asked me to come to her cabin. We went off hand-in-hand, got to her cabin, and as soon as we got in the door began to take each other's clothes off. We must've made love four or five times and I left her cabin about four in the morning. All I remember is that she sucked my dick slowly and deeply, even taking my balls into her mouth and keeping them there until I came. I screamed like a baby! Most men melt under the spell of a good blowjob and I was no exception.

Later that day I was leaving the ship to go to Barbados for training on another vessel. She was continuing on with her family to the end of the cruise in Miami. Before I left her cabin, she gave me her phone number and address on a small piece of paper and asked me to call her when I got back. I reluctantly left her, went back to my cabin, packed my gear and departed the ship in St. Maarten, then headed to Barbados.

It was a Wednesday morning and I was going to be back in Miami on Friday. She wasn't getting back to Miami until Saturday and then she was flying back to Minnesota directly after they disembarked the vessel.

When I returned to Fort Lauderdale and my office on Saturday, I arranged for flowers to be sent to her apartment upon her return. I had two dozen red roses sent and they were to arrive late Saturday afternoon. I made the assumption that she should be getting home by then and I was right. Little did I know her boyfriend Scott, actually her fiancé, was picking her and her family up from the airport when they landed and bringing them all home.

After he had dropped her family off, Tamara and Scott went to her apartment. When they arrived, the roses were in front of her door and she acted as if it was a mistake and that the roses were supposed to be delivered to the apartment next door. Her boyfriend met her at the airport with a single rose that was wilting. To this day, Tamara has laughed about this.

I waited a day and then called her on Monday. She was working at Walgreens and couldn't talk that much, but thanked me for the roses and told me how beautiful they were. I told Tamara that I thought we had something special and I was going to come to visit her in Minnesota. Her schedule was such that she worked for seven nights at Walgreens and then she was off for seven days. I made arrangements to fly to Minnesota the following week when she was off.

Unbeknownst to me, she went through a great deal of trouble to make sure Scott, her boyfriend, was out of town and her mother made sure that her apartment was clean. Apparently, I had all the attributes that Scott did not have and I think they felt I would be a better fit for

Tamara. The mother thought Scott was a loser and she was promoting me to Tamara for the rest of the cruise after I left.

When I arrived in Minnesota, Tamara came to pick me up and she looked beautiful. We went to the Mall of America and then to go eat. I remember it was very cold when I went up there. I still felt very comfortable when I was around her and knew we seemed to have a kindred spirit. I stayed with her for four days, sightseeing in downtown Minneapolis and going back to her apartment and making love. This was something that was going to last a long time. At least that was what I thought...

When I left, I invited her to come to Florida the next time she had her seven days off. I made sure my cruise schedule enabled me to have the time to be with her. We stayed on the beach at Fort Lauderdale, going swimming every day, having drinks, and just enjoying being with each other. The feelings we had for each other just seemed to grow and grow.

During that trip, we also went down to Shooters on the Intracoastal Waterway and that became one of our favorite hangouts. After Tamara went back to Minnesota, we got in the habit of her coming to Florida when she was off and actually going on cruises with me all over the Caribbean. We went on over 35 cruises together all over the world. On one of the cruises, she took her son with us. She entertained him while I did training on the ship, then they transferred us to another vessel. It was really cool that we got to see all the exotic islands in the Caribbean chain. Apparently, Tamara had a double life going on just like I did... Maybe that's why I found her so attractive?

CHAPTER 15

When Tamara was back in Minnesota, she was seeing Scott, and she would tell him she had different types of pharmaceutical training courses that were given in different cities that she had to take when she was off. He believed her, so she was free to come and go as she pleased. Little did he know, she was either heading to Ft. Lauderdale or flying into an exotic port to join me on another cruise.

They had been going together for several years and Tamara was a single mother who had a son, and he was a single father and had a daughter. This seemed to be their common denominator as they did things together with the kids because both kids were approximately the same age. Scott's daughter loved Tamara and Tamara's son looked at Scott like a father. The funny thing is that even at seven, Tamara coached Derek, her son, into not revealing that she was seeing Scott while she was seeing me. The kid was pretty smart and listened to his mother.

My affair with Tamara began in March 1997 and continued until August. During that time, Tamara managed to go on some very romantic cruises with me. After my training on one cruise, we spent a week in Honolulu. We drove around the island, hiked up Diamond Head, ate fruit plates with fresh pineapple, and got naked on the balcony on the 26th floor of the Radisson Hotel in broad daylight. Tamara would say, "Just do me, John," so I did, again and again, as I would squeeze drops of papaya juice and other fruits into her belly button, creating a puddle, that I could lick and suck out before we made love. This especially turned her on because it was such a "teaser."

In June 1997, Tamara invited me to attend her sister's wedding with her in Minnesota, which I accepted. When I got there, Scott was in the back of the church and then in the back of the reception hall, drunk, and running around telling everyone how he loved her and that he was going to kill me. At this point, Scott knew that I was in the picture and didn't like it one bit.

When I left Minnesota after the wedding, Tamara said she was breaking up with Scott, but I didn't believe it. When I got back to Fort Lauderdale, I hired a private detective to watch her and sure enough, right after she dropped me off at the airport and got home, Scott was waiting there in her apartment. The detective got them on camera taking their clothes off, making love—basically having a great time. I was crushed when I got the news. I confronted Tamara and told her I was breaking up with her if she did not break up with Scott. She never gave me an answer so I did not call her anymore. Now it was late June and I was out of touch with Tamara. Holland America was sending me to Juneau, Alaska, in July for one week to do training on six vessels. At this point I figured that was the end of it with me and Tamara.

When I got to Juneau, which was a long plane ride, I was sick with a broken heart thinking that I would not see Tamara ever again. At that point, I came up with a pretty wild plan. I decided that I would buy Tamara a very large engagement ring while I was in Alaska and then fly to Minnesota without her knowing it, find her, propose to her, and give her an ultimatum. The only problem was that I was still married to Kristen. Now what should I do? I knew I loved Tamara, but I also knew I had a family and the responsibilities that went along with it.

Kristen and the kids lived in a neighborhood called Forest Ridge and we lived a pretty decent life. Other than the fact that I was gone a lot, everybody had everything they needed. Kristen worked at the police department, took care of the boys with all of their activities, and I traveled the world. I literally only came and went and was home for maybe one or two days at a time. I was basically an absentee father and husband. My relationship with Kristen was not good to begin with, but now we were only going through the motions.

After a good deal of research, I determined, with help from a very high-profile San Diego divorce attorney, that I could obtain a one-party divorce without the other party ever knowing about it. With that, I flew to San Diego, was taken to Mexico and stood up in front of a Mexican judge. The attorney spoke in Spanish and the next thing you know, I was divorced. It cost me $2000, which included the payoff to the judge. The judge was even kind enough to backdate the divorce to 1992.

The theory behind this one-party divorce was that as long as it wasn't contested, it would stand. At the time, I was heavily in debt and everything was leveraged. While I made a lot of money, I also spent a lot of money maintaining everyone's lifestyle, including my own. The attorney in San Diego told me I had nothing to lose by giving it a shot and, if for some reason my wife wanted to challenge the divorce, she would have to pay and prove that it was bogus. I went ahead with it and the divorce decree was issued and mailed to me upon my return to Florida.

Kristen never knew that we were divorced and as far as I was concerned, we were. Very twisted, I know.

I purchased a beautiful ring with a gigantic two-carat diamond for Tamara while I was in Juneau. It was a custom piece that was one of a kind. It took the jeweler two days to get it ready and at the end of my training sessions, instead of flying back to Florida, I flew directly to O'Hare in Chicago. From O'Hare, I rented a car and drove nine hours to Minneapolis.

It was a Saturday and I had called her mother and told her about my whole plan to show up at her apartment and propose to her. Her mother told me that Tamara and her family would be attending a wedding that day in northern Minnesota and they would all be back around six that evening. That worked out perfectly in that I arrived in Minneapolis about an hour before they came back. I waited in the parking lot of Tamara's apartment complex until her parents showed up and dropped her off. That weekend her son was with his father, so she had no one there. For some reason, Scott was not around and at that point I wasn't sure why.

When Tamara's parents dropped her off, I waited for about ten minutes until she got into the apartment. Then I went to her door, knocked on it, and she almost died to see me standing there. She was in shock that I had actually gone through all that trouble to get there from Alaska. As soon as I got inside, I got on my knee and proposed to her. I pulled out the ring and placed it on her finger and she was speechless.

Just at that moment, Scott called her. It turned out he was on maneuvers for the weekend with his squadron. She answered the phone and told him very directly that I was there and I had just proposed to her and she had accepted. He was crushed and he was screaming and crying on the phone. She simply hung up on him and proceeded to kiss me which turned into a two-hour lovemaking session.

We spent the whole weekend together, going out to eat and going home to make love. We made many plans during that weekend and then I left to go back to Fort Lauderdale.

On the way back to Fort Lauderdale, I was completely confused as to how I was going to handle this. I had obtained the one-party divorce, but for all practical purposes, I was still married to Kristen. Tamara was going to come to Florida on her next cycle off so we could look for houses and I had to rearrange my schedule so I was off while she was there, then tell Kristen I was going on a cruise. This was a very difficult juggling act to say the least.

Tamara came in the following week and we began to look for houses. We looked in Coral Springs and Fort Lauderdale. We looked all over the place including Weston Hills. We found a beautiful home in Weston Hills and decided that was the one. We purchased the house and began to make plans to get married. I managed to pull off Tamara coming for the week, then leaving. When she left and I went home to my house in Forest Ridge, it was clear this was going to become very stressful for me, but I was in it now with no turning back. When I went to my office the following Monday, I clued Judy in on everything and she agreed to help me live a double life.

Tamara and I agreed that she would give me $50,000 as part of her contribution for the house. We planned on getting married in September and prior to that she would go on an incredible cruise with me before we got married; then, after we were married, would go on a whirlwind trip to Europe for our honeymoon.

The week came and we got married at Burt & Jack's in Fort Lauderdale. We had a beautiful ceremony in the garden and then we had a wonderful dinner. Two people we had met on a cruise served as our witnesses and they attended the dinner with us, as no family was present. We hired a limousine to drive us up and down Fort Lauderdale Beach and we eventually ended up at the Hilton, where we spent a honeymoon weekend. Right after that, Tamara and I had to part because she had to go back to work and I had to go on a short cruise to do additional training.

The following week we headed off to Europe. I told Kristen I was going on a trip overseas to do training on several vessels. This was obviously something that I did often, so she didn't ask any questions.

I flew to Orlando and met Tamara who came in from Minnesota and from there we both flew to Amsterdam.

We had an incredible time in Amsterdam taking in all the sights including the Van Gogh Museum, the works of Rembrandt, the Heineken brewery, as well as Anne Frank's house. We sailed on the canals and drank Voss beer. We walked through the red-light district and enjoyed all the sights of the city. We stayed in a great boutique hotel called the Mercury Inn.

The airlines had lost Tamara's luggage and we had to stay an extra day to wait for them to deliver her bag to the hotel. She had no clean underwear or fresh clothes. Once we got her bag, we were free to travel. We rented a Rover sedan and then began our journey from Amsterdam to Antwerp, Belgium to Paris. We passed through Rotterdam, had coffee in Brussels, then on to Antwerp, and drove into Paris at midnight. It was fabulous!

Once we got into Paris, we got lost and it was very late and I had no idea where I was going. We went through several tunnels and wound up at a hotel right near the Arc de Triumph called the Hotel Americana. It was now about one-thirty in the morning and I went to the desk and asked how much it was for the night. They said five hundred American dollars and I said, "No problem, I will take it."

While I was at the desk, the car was parked outside with Tamara in it. She had to move the car while I was inside and she accidentally hit all the cement barriers outside of the hotel. She essentially dented the entire side of the car! It was so late and I was so tired that I went back to the car on the driver's side, gave the keys to the valet, took the luggage, and had no idea as to what happened. Tamara knew, but she didn't say anything. We checked into the room and both fell asleep. We didn't wake up until ten o'clock the next morning.

Out the window, we had a panoramic view of Paris. We could see the Eiffel Tower and everything in a 180° radius. It was breathtaking. We made love, got ready, had a great breakfast, and then headed out to walk all over the city. We walked through the Arc de Triumph, then down to the Cathedral of Notre Dame, went on a tour of the Louvre, and walked to the Seine River, and then walked five miles to the Eiffel Tower.

We arrived at the Eiffel Tower just as it was getting dark. While we were up in the tower, we saw the lights of Paris come on. It was a very romantic moment.

We had dinner in the Eiffel Tower and then went to the top. By this time it was eleven o'clock and we went back to the hotel to go to sleep. The next morning, we left Paris and headed to Calais, France. Our intention was to take the ferry to England, but when we got close there were signs saying that we could take the Chunnel under the English Channel and I decided to go that way.

All of this time, I had no idea that the car was dented on the passenger side. For whatever reason, I just didn't look. It didn't seem to affect the way the car drove, so I had no idea. When we got to the Chunnel, we had to go through security, and then we drove the car onto the train. The train took off and got up to 128 miles an hour as we went under the English Channel. We arrived in Dover about thirty-five minutes later and got up onto the M4 heading toward London.

On the way to London, we stopped at Henry VIII's castle and went sightseeing. It was a real castle with a moat and everything else, just like in the movies. Once we left the castle, we headed into London where we wound up at Trafalgar Square and, amazingly, found a place to park. Once parked, we walked to Buckingham Palace, down the street to Big Ben and the Red Lion pub, Piccadilly Circus, and Number 10 Downing Street.

We had lunch at some great restaurants and managed to see a good bit of London. At that time, Princess Diana had recently been killed and all the flowers were still in front of Buckingham Palace. We got to see that as well as the changing of the guard. It was all memorable to say the least.

At the end of the day, we got back in the car and drove over the Queen Elizabeth Bridge back to the Chunnel train station where we drove the car onto the train and headed back to France. We got to France about midnight and everything was closed. We found a hotel and started banging on the door and the innkeeper turned the lights on and was kind enough to let us in and give us a room.

In the morning when I came out, I finally got to see the damage on the car. I freaked out and Tamara denied everything. She said she had no idea what happened. Regardless, we had to get back to the airport in Amsterdam to return the car and make our flight. We hauled ass all the way back through France and Holland and made it to the airport several hours before our flight was to depart back to the United States. At the car return, they charged me $5000 for the damage and I had to put it on my American Express card.

We flew back to Orlando. She went back to Minnesota and I went back to Fort Lauderdale. Although we were married, this back and forth went on until July. I was getting the Weston Hills house ready for her arrival, but I was still going on my cruises and maintaining my other family. Tamara came down every other week and we would either go to the beach, to the new house, or to the apartment that I had rented on the Intracoastal.

Needless to say, for as much money as I was making, I was spending it like water. I decorated the house in Weston to the ninth degree. It was done in all ivory and gold with a baby grand piano to boot. It looked like Liberace should live there! The window treatments alone cost over $28,000 and all the furniture was imported from Italy. I dropped over

$150,000 into our dream house. In addition, I bought her a brand-new BMW convertible that I parked in the garage. It was red with a gray leather interior. It was a knockout car!

All of this time, she had no idea how I was decorating the house. She was making plans to move from Minnesota and had to arrange everything for her replacement at Walgreens. Upon her arrival in Florida, she would not be able to work at a pharmacy because Minnesota and Florida did not have reciprocity in licensing. She had to study and take the state boards all over again before she could work.

Finally, the day came in 1997 when she flew to Florida for the last time. She came with her cat and her work clothes, thinking that she would have to paint and redecorate the house. But it had all been done for her already. When I picked her up at the airport, I blindfolded her, took her out to the house, and, upon opening the garage door, pulled the blindfold off. She saw a beautiful house with a brand-new red BMW in the garage.

When she went inside, she was shocked to see that every single thing was taken care of, including plates, silverware, glasses, and everything else. She was speechless. The following week I arranged it so I would stay with her the first week while she was there, but then had to go on a cruise when she left. Now things were getting a little dicey because my other family lived only eight miles away and I had to juggle things between both locations.

I managed to pull this off pretty handily with the help of Judy. I was always on the move so nobody knew where I was. At that time, cell phone service was sketchy, so being contacted wasn't that easy. I was able to successfully lead a double life for over two years with nobody knowing the difference. I had another name, "Jimmy," and I had the gate guards in the community paid off so they would protect my cover. I had several cars hiding in different places around town. The windows were tinted and they were all parked in underground garages so no one could see me coming and going. It was like being Batman. The whole thing gave me an incredible rush! The adrenaline always seemed to be pumping!

Tamara studied for the boards, took the test, and passed. She was very smart—I had no doubt she would pass. She took a job working at night at a wholesale pharmacy near the house, so she worked all night and slept all day. This made it easy for me in that I would go see my other family, go on cruises, go back to my family, then go see Tamara. This without a doubt took its toll on me.

Because Tamara's schedule was the complete reverse of mine and I traveled so much, she began to make friends and do things without me. I was gone a lot and I didn't like the company she was keeping. She took up scuba diving and was always out with the guys that were in her class. She was off all day and they all would go out early in the morning diving and not come back until mid afternoon. Many times, they would go over to my house and would go in my pool. I'm sure there was some hanky-panky going on as well, but who was I to talk?

All of this continued on until the fall of 1997. While still close, Tamara and I seemed to be drifting apart. I was feeling more and more guilty about my family and seemed to be going home to them more than to the house in Weston. Tamara had her friends and always seemed to have a party going on. I was not a party person and I did not like the skin diving. I had nothing in common with any of the people she knew. I was always coming and going and preparing for cruises. I found everything they did frivolous and wanted nothing to do with them.

One day I came home to Weston and, much to my surprise as I walked to the door, I looked into the bedroom and I could see Tamara naked, sitting on top of a guy, going up and down. They were clasping each other's hands and she would let out a little scream on each down stroke. She had on his airline captain's hat and turned around, looked at me and said, "What are you doing here?" Then she continued to ride the guy. It turned out that he was an airline captain for Continental that she had met when she was on a flight back from visiting Minnesota. His name was Captain Jack. As soon as I saw what she was doing, I turned around and left.

I went home to my family and the next day went to my office and filed for divorce from her. I went to a lawyer in Fort Lauderdale and he prepared the papers. It was now November 1997, and we both went to court in early December and the divorce was granted. I had to give her $50,000 back and she, in turn, relieved herself of any claim on the house. That was that.

Immediately she moved out and got an apartment down on Hallandale Beach about 20 miles away. While I was divorced from Tamara, I was still for all practical purposes still married to Kristen. My lawyer told me I was nuts and that I was a bigamist, but now that I was divorced, the situation was resolved, unless someone found out about it, which I was careful that no one did.

I helped Tamara move to her new apartment and then I had the entire Weston house sanitized, so it was completely clean and like new before Christmas of 1997. Tamara was now gone and I was going to give my marriage to Kristen another try, for the fourth time.

On Christmas Eve of 1997, I told Kristen I had a great Christmas present for her and the kids. I put a paper bag on her head and took her out to Weston and then when we were right in front of the house, asked her to take it off. She was speechless!! I told her the house had been purchased for her and that it was a new beginning for us. The kids knew all about the whole thing with Tamara and they agreed not to blow my cover. I also had to go to all the neighbors and let them know not to mention anything about Tamara ever being there. They complied, but thought that I was a flake. Do you blame them?

In January 1998, we sold our Davie house and Kristen and the kids moved to Weston.

Tamara was now in Hallandale Beach and I continued to see her on and off. You know how you can't stay away from someone you loved after they're gone? It's kind of weird, but now we were more attracted to each other than ever, and I found myself going to visit Tamara all the time. The sex was also fantastic!

In February 1998, I drove Tamara and her son all the way to Minnesota so she could visit her family and spend several months there. I did it and then flew back to Florida. Now that I look back at it, it was crazy! When Tamara came back to Florida, I went over to see her one night and, as I walked through the door, I tripped over somebody's shoes and they weren't hers. I looked in the bedroom and there was a guy sleeping with her. With that, I quietly left and didn't call her anymore. To this day, she still lives with that guy in Pompano Beach. They have been together for almost eighteen years.

After Kristen and the kids moved into the new house, I knew this was probably a mistake. Kristen's and my relationship wasn't much better; it was clear she did not like the long drive back to Plantation to her job at the police department. It was twenty-five miles one way and there was always a traffic jam.

I was still going on cruises and after Tamara I met even more women, lots more. I had spent so much money fixing the house up and buying the yacht that I was spending a lot more than I was taking in. I could still afford it, but felt moving out was the best thing to do. We downsized and moved into a small condominium much closer to Kristen's job and to Port Everglades where my office was located.

In April of 1998 we moved out of the Weston house, rented it out and saved ourselves a bunch of money. I rented the house for $3500 a month, but that barely covered the mortgage and expenses. The people stayed in the house for only a few months. The house stayed vacant for a very long time. When we moved, I sold all the furniture in an estate sale and everything was gone in a matter of hours. Once the renters left, I resumed paying the mortgage.

I was bored with Kristen as usual and started a year-and-a-half run with more women that made Hugh Hefner seem like an altar boy!

CHAPTER 16

The cruise lines continued to send me all over, to some very exotic places, and everywhere I went, there were more and more adventures with beautiful women in all different walks of life and from many different nationalities—Russians, Asians, Scandinavians, even women from Iceland. There were so many, I could barely keep up.

The cruise lines were building three or four new ships a year, each one bigger and better than the next. They were magnificent vessels with incredible amenities and beautiful designs. In the beginning, every cruise was exciting and the experiences were incredible. I went to all the ports in the Caribbean, all the way down to South America. They sent me to Barcelona and all over the Mediterranean. I went to Norway, Denmark, Finland, and even St. Petersburg, Russia. Then they sent me to the Far East, Hong Kong, Thailand, and Singapore, sailing up and down the Asian coast, then to New Zealand.

I met women on every cruise. I even met one girl right after she got married. We were sitting on the deck of the *Norway* where I was having lunch in my uniform. She was still in her wedding dress. She sat at my table and I said "Congratulations."

She said, "For what?"

I said, "Didn't you just get married?"

She said, "Yes, but my husband's an asshole."

I asked, "Why?"

She said he just was and she was sorry and that as soon as the cruise was over, she was getting divorced.

I said, "Did you consummate the marriage yet?"

She said, "What does that mean?"

I don't know what possessed me to say it, but I said, "Never mind, do you want to fuck?"

She said, "Sure, I would love to!"

I got up and said, "Follow me." We walked single file back to my cabin. When we got in the room, she lifted up her bridal gown and pulled her underwear off. She even left her veil on.

I pounded the shit out of her. She had a big orgasm, then lit up a cigarette and said, "Thanks, needed that." Then she left.

I never saw her again on the whole cruise. But it was a real turn on fucking a newly married bride with her wedding gown still on. She also left her white shoes on, even better! That was a wild one!

Another time, I was sent to Guadalupe by Carnival to board a ship for training. As soon as I got on the ship, I went to the Lido deck while the ship was getting ready to pull away. I was standing next to a tall, good-looking, dark-haired beauty from Texas. Her name was Rita Decker—that one I remember.

As the ship pulled out, I asked her if she would like to have a wine with me. She said OK, but she wasn't going back to my cabin. I said OK.

Within twenty minutes, we were in my cabin, in the middle of the afternoon and she was naked and sitting on my cock. She rode me hard and was yelling the whole time. She only wanted to sit on me. I wasn't going to argue, so we fucked until about ten that night, ordering in food and drinking wine and sitting on the floor. Every half hour or so, she would sit on me again and cum again.

When she left, I did not see her again for the rest of my time on the vessel. I tried to find her after I got back, but never could. There were so many similar stories…each more bizarre than the next…some of them good, and some of them great!

This whole crazy schedule continued throughout 1998 and 1999. The women came and went and in a pinch, I could always go to the Weston house and throw an air mattress on the floor. It was clean and spacious, but empty. I kept a few things there, but not much. If I did go there, it was under the cover of darkness, so the neighbors, who thought I was nuts anyway, wouldn't see me as I zipped in and out of the garage.

During this time, business picked up and the money was flowing like water with no slowdown in sight. I thought about moving out of the condominium we were living in, but then I decided against it. That turned out to be a good decision for a variety of reasons.

In the summer of 1999, Costa sent me to live in Genoa, Italy, for three months. I lived in the Columbus Hotel down near the port and boarded a different vessel every week to train the crew members on every ship they had in their fleet. I sailed all over the Mediterranean, leaving out of Genoa and going to France, Sicily, Greece, Africa, and Spain. I especially had a wild time in Majorca, the island off Spain.

When we pulled into the port of Majorca, I was on the *Costa Romantica*. It was a beautiful day and I was off due to scheduling issues with the crew for the training. I was just as glad. I got up early, ate breakfast on the Lido deck, and headed down to the gangway to disembark the vessel and go sightseeing in the city.

It was a gorgeous day and I had no idea what I was about to get into. When I got down to the dock, I hailed a cab and I asked the driver where I could go to have a good time. He knew exactly what I meant and told me he would take me to a place called the Mustang Ranch. I had heard of this, but thought that the only Mustang Ranch was in Nevada. Apparently, there was another one in Majorca, Spain.

The driver took me all over town—past the beautiful cathedral and the bustling shopping district to the outskirts of the island where I saw a mansion all by itself standing next to the sea. He dropped me off, took my twenty bucks, and told me to knock on the door.

I knocked on the door and a lady came to the door and asked me what I was doing there. I told her the cab driver said this was the place where I could have the time of my life. With that, she let me in.

As soon as I entered, there was a small window where a guy immediately asked me what type of credit card I had. I told him I had an American Express card as well as several other credit cards and that's all they had to hear. The lady took my American Express card to hold on file until I left and then I entered the bar area.

It was a beautiful, sumptuous bar, with soft chairs, dim lighting and high-end liquor. Several other men were there with a variety of beautiful women all paying attention to them. As soon as I walked in, several of them came over to me and wanted to know my name, where I was from, what I did, and struck up a very intelligent conversation with me about every subject you can imagine.

At this time, it was about eleven in the morning and the drinks were flowing freely. I had three or four women all hanging around me, fighting for my attention. One was more beautiful than the next and I had a hard time deciding who I wanted to be with. Apparently, this was the way it worked. Four or five women would greet you and then you had several hours to sort out who you wanted to be with. There was no rush because I did not have to be back to the ship until the next morning.

One of the girls asked me if I wanted to go on a tour of the house. I said sure, why not.

She escorted me down some winding halls and showed me several different rooms. These rooms were all theme rooms. One room was like the surface of the moon and had a lunar landing module on it, but that, of course, was a bed. Another room was like the Roman Coliseum with the chariot in the middle of it and that was a bed. Another room was decorated like a pirate ship and in the middle of the deck of the ship was another bed. She asked me what room I liked the best and wanted to know if I wanted her to go with me into whatever room I liked the most. I didn't know what to say.

At this point, several of the women started to follow us around and the next thing you know, because I had been drinking, I invited them to go with me in each one of the rooms. We went crazy! All of them were giving me head, sitting on my face, all sucking me at the same time and making me do them two at a time. I was going insane. When we got done in one room, we would move to another and go through the whole thing all over again. It was completely hedonistic and reminded me of Caligula! By the end of the fourth theme room, I was exhausted and so were they.

We all took a shower. They gave me a massage, and then we all went into an exquisite dining room to eat dinner. The food was fantastic and so was the wine. I was in the company of four of the most beautiful women I had ever been with and every one of them was from a different European country, all educated, well versed in everything, and incredibly intelligent. Not to mention, they were all experts in anything you would ever want to know about sex. They all seemed to like me because of my expert training many years earlier. I don't think any normal man could have kept up with all of them the way that I did.

There was one girl in particular from South America who was truly exquisite. She propositioned me to stay with her the entire night. I asked her how much it would be and she told me $1500. I said that would be fine. We went to another part of the mansion and had our own private bedroom for the rest of the evening.

By this time, it was about ten in the evening and the whole thing started all over again with this beautiful girl from South America. She gave me a bubble bath, a hot stone massage, a long, delightful hand job, sucked on my cock for thirty minutes, knowing just how to bring me to the point of orgasm and then let me go down. After doing this two or three times she finally lay on the bed, opened her legs and told me to put my penis in her, which is exactly what I did. I was so on the edge that I came in three seconds. We made love over and over again for over two hours. The candles were lit, it was cool, we had beautiful sheets, and she smelled wonderful. Her hands were cool and seasoned. She knew just how to handle a man's cock. After this marathon sex session, we fell asleep and did not wake up until about eight the next morning.

By this time, I knew I had to get back to the ship, so I threw myself together, said goodbye to her and went down to exit the mansion. Right by the door was the window where I had left my American Express card. The lady asked me if I wanted to sign out, and I said yes. She handed me the total—over $6000! I signed the bill, took a copy of the receipt, and they called me a taxi.

The taxi took me back to the ship, I boarded it, and we weighed anchor for France. As soon as we got out of the port, I was summoned to the bridge because I had gotten a phone call from my office in the United States. It was my secretary, Judy, who had American Express on the other line back in the office. They wanted to know if I had authorized a $6,000 expenditure in Majorca Spain. I laughed out loud and said, "Tell them yes, it was me."

After Majorca, I trained over nine hundred crew members on the ship and made myself a cool $31,500. So, what was six grand in the big picture? Just a drop in the bucket!

When we got back to port, I disembarked the *Costa Romantica* and went back to the Hotel Colombo. The next day, there were no ships to go on, so I went down to the port into an Italian market and had fresh mozzarella, tomato, and prosciutto sandwiches for lunch. They were fantastic! The rest of the day I lay by the pool, just enjoying the sunshine at the bar in the back of the hotel.

The next morning, I boarded a different Costa vessel, the *Costa Classica*. For the next week, we sailed all around Italy. We left Genoa, sailed to Naples, the Isle of Capri, Rome, and then down to Palermo, Sicily. It was a delightful cruise and when it ended, it concluded my nine-week stay in Genoa, training every crew member on all of the Costa vessels. When I disembarked the ship, I went back to the hotel, packed nine weeks' worth of clothing, and headed off to the airport to fly back to Fort Lauderdale. It had been quite an adventure traveling to all those countries and the various islands all over the Mediterranean on every itinerary that Costa had.

The flight back to Florida was long—I had to connect in Milan to get a direct flight back to Miami. It took me about twelve hours to get back. When I came home, I was exhausted, but I had to get back to my office in order to invoice Costa for the nine weeks' worth of training. The total bill for my services was in excess of $200,000. Though I was tired, the very next day I was in the office and Judy was sending the invoices to Costa headquarters in Italy for payment.

CHAPTER 17

Because I had been gone so long, I had purposely delayed setting up training on any additional ships just so I could get readjusted to East Coast time again and get my feet back on the ground. I was also buying a house for my mother and father out in Weston Hills, very close to where my house was.

I met a girl at the title company who seemed to like me. She had one hell of a body and everybody could just not help staring at her. Her face wasn't the greatest, but her body was killer. She had great legs and you could tell her pussy was hungry. Her toes were perfect and she smelled fresh and clean. Her hair was short and her mouth was wide. I could tell she knew how to suck it, just by looking at her. Her whole aura was sexual, short skirts and open-toed shoes all the time. Her big toe was always spread apart from her second toe. My experience told me that she was a "toe grabber" when she was getting laid, hanging onto her big toes for better leverage, so she could fuck her partner back and get his pecker deep inside of her.

During the process of buying a home for my parents, she had to come to my office several times. On more than one occasion, she would accidentally drop something and then squat down to pick it up. It was clear she had no underwear on and she basically wanted to let me know that she didn't. As usual I couldn't help myself and I asked her to go to dinner.

We went on several dates, but I just wasn't sure if we had any kind of a connection in spite of the fact that she had such a great body. One particular Sunday, she asked me if I would like to go with her to Shooters to meet her stepmother, a lady named Jane. She had located her after many years and this was going to be a reunion meeting of sorts. I accepted the invitation and went to Shooters to meet up with her stepmother. We arrived first and then Jane walked into the room.

She was a little woman with a very beautiful face and petite body to match. She looked just like Jane Wyman. Her smile, her hairdo, everything about her was classy and attractive to me. I could see in her eyes as we sat across the table from each other that she liked me, also. We couldn't stop staring at each other and when her daughter went to the bathroom, I looked her right in the eye and asked her if she would like to go out with me.

She spoke with a "Texicana" accent because she lived in Houston. This made her even more attractive. At first, she said, "Oh my, that wouldn't be right to do," but then she accepted. She said she'd be in town several more days and told me what hotel she was staying at.

When her daughter returned, we continued to have our lunch and make small talk and eventually we said our goodbyes. The daughter went off with her to reminisce and I went home.

I couldn't wait to contact Jane that evening to ask her when we could get together. I went home to Kristen and I actually fell asleep and did not call Jane until the following morning. She immediately answered the phone in the room and was concerned that I hadn't called her the night before. She thought she had done something wrong. I said no, I just fell asleep and it got so late that I decided not to call her until today. She was relieved and asked when we could get together. I immediately asked her if she wanted to have lunch. She said yes, of course.

We agreed to meet at one that afternoon. She asked me to come to her hotel on 17th Street to pick her up. I showed up in my little Mercedes and she looked beautiful as she came out of the lobby, dressed in a cute little dress, beautiful red toenails, bright red lipstick, and just a gorgeous look. I was getting excited gazing at her. We went across the street to the Bimini boatyard and had lunch.

We chit-chatted for about three hours, and then she asked me to take her back to the hotel. She asked me if I would like to go up to her room, and I said sure. As soon as we got to the door, we started kissing passionately and then she asked me if we were going to have sex. She said it in a little schoolgirl voice that really turned me on.

She said to take it easy on her because she hadn't had sex in a long time. With that I slowly removed her clothes, pulled down her panties, and went down on her. She was squirming and screaming and all of a sudden began to talk very dirty. Her voice dropped down two octaves. She asked me multiple times to give her a real good fucking and asked me if I wanted her to open her pussy up with her red finger nails, so I could see it in the light. Finally, I stuck it in and she squirted all over the place. She had a huge orgasm and began speaking like a little whore.

It was funny. When I first met her, she said she attended church every Sunday and sang in the choir. Go figure. She sang all right! When I said it was time for me to go, she asked why. I said I had to go to my son's ball game. She reluctantly said goodbye and asked me to come to Houston. I said, OK, in a couple of weeks.

With that, I left and went home and after the house closed for my parents, never did find out if Natalie grabbed her toes or not, but I was sure she did.

CHAPTER 18

When I got home, I went to my son's ball game and then went back home and lay on the couch to watch TV for the rest of the day. Jane called me and left me several messages that she had taken off on time from Fort Lauderdale airport and had landed in Houston. I was tired and stayed quiet the rest of the evening, then went to bed.

When I woke up that morning I felt fine, had a couple cups of coffee and then began to do my exercises. Usually I did a hundred jumping jacks, a hundred sit-ups, and jogged in place for fifteen to twenty minutes. I started doing my jumping jacks, and suddenly I got a sharp pain across my chest going from left to right. It stopped me right in my tracks!

My hands felt weak and I had to lie down. I wasn't sure what was wrong, but I knew something was very wrong. This weak feeling in my hands and my body prompted me to go to the hospital where they immediately gave me an EKG and checked all my vitals to see if I had had a heart attack. Everything seemed normal, but then the doctor said that he wanted me to take a stress test. They sent me over to the clinic next door. I had to wait for about an hour before they called me in and hooked me up with all the wires and started the test.

Everything was going fine about six minutes into the test. Then, when they started to accelerate the machine, I had a heart attack right on the machine with the doctor and his assistant in front of me. They immediately stopped the test, laid me on the table, and said that it looked like from the EKG I had some kind of a blockage that had resulted a minor heart attack! Within minutes I found myself on a gurney being wheeled back to the hospital and into the Cath Lab for an immediate angiogram and possible angioplasty or stent placement. I was scared to death and did not know what to expect.

As I lay on the gurney waiting to go into the Cath Lab, a million things flashed in my head. Everything I had done, the crazy life I was living and the insane schedule that I had to juggle while living all these different lives. It seemed like an eternity had gone by when a nurse finally came in and said, "We're going to give you a needle in your groin. That will dull the pain for when we place the shunt that will enable the doctor to insert the catheter into your femoral artery which will go up to your heart." She also told me that I would be conscious the whole time and that I would be asked to move from side to side as the medical team maneuvered the catheter through my arteries.

Before they gave me the Lidocaine shot, a nurse shaved my entire pubic area and then they gave me the needle. It pinched, but it did not hurt too badly, so I said to myself, "How bad can this be?"

About ten minutes went by. Then several nurses appeared and put a small white curtain up so I couldn't see my groin area. The next thing I felt was a huge needle being plunged into my groin with blood shooting out all over the place. The pain was unbelievable in spite of the Lidocaine shot. It felt like the needle went six inches down into my groin and thigh. Within a few moments the nurses were able to control the bleeding and they capped it like an oil well.

They had placed the shunt into my femoral artery. Next we waited for the doctors to wheel me into the lab so they could perform the procedure. I was so scared that I started to shake.

Before I knew it, I was on the operating table and they were inserting the catheter into my body. There were several large television sets on the wall and they told me to look at the screen so I could see just how the catheter was wiggling its way right up through my arteries to my heart. They told me to move from side to side and roll over, as they continued to insert the catheter into the various blood vessels.

It was very clear that there were several blockages that stopped the catheter on its journey. I could see them on the screen and so could they. At that point they pulled the catheter out, put stents on the end, and then reinserted it. They use a balloon to expand the artery and placed the stent and then they moved the catheter back out. It was amazing to see how the blood began to flow freely immediately.

They determined that two of my arteries were seriously blocked and needed stents. One stent was placed in the elbow of what is known as the "widow maker." The widow maker is the artery that usually kills men when they have a blockage in that area. I was lucky enough that the stent could be placed without bypass surgery.

After the procedure, I was admitted to the hospital for several days to recover. My enzyme levels were also elevated and this was something that the doctors were concerned about. I was not getting out of that hospital until my enzyme levels had gone back down to normal.

The doctor could not understand why a seemingly healthy, active person like me had had a heart attack. One night he came in and asked me, "Lazano, what's up with you? You should not be like this."

I told him I had five girlfriends from all over, a secret double life and a yacht.

He said, "OK, now, I understand. Christ, no wonder you're blocked up! That alone is enough to give anyone a heart attack!

During this time, Kristen, my kids, my mother and father, and Judy, my secretary, were all at the hospital waiting while I was being treated. This all happened on a Sunday so everyone was off and it was a relatively quiet day. Since Jane had returned to Houston, I hadn't heard from her, but it had only been a day.

I had my cell phone with me in my room and it was turned off until everyone left in the evening. Sure enough, on Sunday evening, Jane called and I was able to answer the phone. She had called three or four times. Each time her message was more frantic, wondering why I didn't answer the phone.

On Monday morning, she called my office. Judy had taken the day off to come to the hospital so we had a temp in the office. When Jane called, the temp told her I was in the hospital and had had a heart attack. What an idiot! Now Jane was calling the hospital wanting to be connected to my room. Everyone was around me constantly and I couldn't take her calls.

When Kristen left the room, I asked Judy to call her back and tell her I was in the hospital, but wasn't able to speak to anyone. Judy took care of that but Jane in Houston didn't buy it. She started asking a million questions and then wanted to fly back to Fort Lauderdale to visit me and take care of me. Of course, she didn't know I was married.

At the same time and during that week several of the women I had been involved with called the office. The temp told them I was unavailable and in the hospital. This was a big mistake! Several of them started calling all the local hospitals and found out where I was.

By the third day, I was deluged with phone calls, gifts, and flowers, all coming to the hospital—all for me. My son Sergio had to stand in the lobby and wait for the florist to come so he could intercept the flowers and have them sent to hospice. I also had Judy go to all the nurses' stations and essentially pay them off to not forward any calls to my room.

The whole hospital was in an uproar because I was there and the word was getting around about what I was up to. Finally, after seven days, my enzyme levels went down to normal and I was discharged. Even though I felt weak, I immediately got in my car and drove right to the office to see what was going on and what I had missed. Judy had kept everything pretty tight as she went to the office every night to keep track of things and the temp answered the phone during the day. As soon as I went to the office, I returned all the phone calls of everyone who had called me and let them know I was okay and not to worry. Jane was extremely upset in that she felt I was dodging her and, of course, she was right. Regardless, she said she still wanted me to go to Houston to visit her when I was well enough and she felt that she loved me. I didn't get a hard-on once while I was in the hospital, so I was about due. Although, I must admit, I was scared to death having sex again would surely kill me, but I was willing to try.

The cruise lines wanted me to go on several cruises right after I got out of the hospital, but I delayed them for two weeks while I recovered. I went to the beach, trying to relax, but the burning desire for excitement started to creep up on me again as I felt stronger and stronger. Apparently, the blockages I had had been slowing me down a little, but now the blood was flowing at full speed.

After two weeks of hanging around the office and going down to the beach, Holland America sent me an email asking me to do a new round of training on twelve ships, one week after another, with itineraries that sailed everywhere. I eagerly accepted the assignment and was off again.

The first ship I sailed on again was the *Massdam*. It sailed out of Fort Lauderdale and went to the Caribbean. I trained over a thousand people in one week and made $35,000! Not bad for a week's work! I didn't need to get involved with any women on this cruise; I was just getting my strength back and beginning to feel my oats again. The heart attack did scare me, but I felt that everything had been corrected and I was back in full form by the end of the cruise.

The next cruise wasn't scheduled for two weeks, so I had some time to go to visit Jane in Houston if that's what I wanted to do. The following weekend, I told Kristen I was going on a cruise out of the port of Houston and instead I went to visit Jane at her home.

She met me at the airport and gave me a big sensuous, loving kiss and said how much she was worried about me and that she missed me. I got there late in the afternoon. It was a typical rainy summer afternoon in Houston with high humidity. She took me back to her house by way of the 610 loop; it was off Westheimer, all the way on the west side of town. We had a romantic dinner in a little restaurant right on Wertheimer and then went back to her house.

It was probably about seven-thirty when we got home. She immediately went and took a shower, then came out of the bathroom with a little robe on and nothing else. She smelled delicious with a sensual perfume that she had sprayed on herself right after the shower. She turned the dim light on in her bedroom and then I took a shower while she waited in the living room for me to be finished.

When I came out of the shower, she was standing in the dim light of her bedroom and slowly opened her robe. Her petite body was beautiful and her pussy was shaved and she looked like she was full of desire. I had just finished drying off and walked into the bedroom naked when she just got down on her knees and began to give me a slow and deep blowjob. She got into it and was huffing and puffing and then started to talk dirty as she had done in Fort Lauderdale when I left her. Apparently, this got her very excited.

After she sucked on my cock for a while, she made me lie down in bed and then she sat on top of me and told me to fuck her good, like the bad girl that she was. She liked being bad! Her eyes were rolling back in her head as she rode me like a bucking bronco.

After she was out of breath, she rolled over and laid down on her back, spread her legs wide open and instructed me to stick it in as deep as I could. I did and she hung onto her ankles while I banged her for at least 30 minutes straight. I was afraid of my heart giving out, considering what I had just gone through. When she came, she started screaming and squirting all over the place. When she started doing that, I could not help but come just like her. We both were making a lot of noise.

When we were done, we just lay there panting and catching our breath. We started talking about it and the next thing you know we were doing it for a second round. This time all she wanted me to do was give it to her in the missionary position and she loved it. She came at least three more times and I had nothing left in me for a fourth round. I was exhausted. I fell asleep and so did she.

The next day, for whatever reason, I was feeling guilty. I decided I needed to leave, so I pretended to receive a call from Holland America saying that I had to get back to Fort Lauderdale to sail out on the ship the following day. This was my excuse to leave that afternoon.

Jane was very upset and could not understand why I had to leave so soon. I told her it was my job, but she did not want to hear it. Regardless, I managed to get a flight that afternoon out of Hobby Airport back to Fort Lauderdale. She took me to the airport, dropped me off, and said call her when I wanted to see her again. She basically wanted me to ask her to come back to Fort Lauderdale so we could hang out and she could see her long-lost daughter again. When I got out of the car at the curb, I was relieved and glad to be boarding the flight.

Once I was seated and the flight took off, I noticed a beautiful woman sitting right in front of me. I was standing up in the aisle after we reached cruising altitude, but the only things I could see initially were her toes and the beautiful sandals that she had on. Beautiful toes just turn me on and make me melt.

I was still standing behind her and I could see her hair was in a bun and pulled back very tight. She had sunglasses on and a loosely fitting sundress. I wasn't quite sure what to say, but I said it anyway. I tapped her on the shoulder and said, "You really have beautiful feet."

She turned around and her face was just as lovely as her feet. She said thank you and I found out her name was Helen. She said she was visiting Fort Lauderdale for about a week to see some friends and then she was heading back to Houston to her parents' house and then back to Maui, Hawaii, where she lived.

It turned out she was a minister who performed weddings in Maui. That was a job. We talked with each other the whole flight back and, before you know it, we were landing in Fort Lauderdale. I asked her for her number and we made a date to have dinner one night while she was in town so we could get to know each other better. Her friends greeted her upon her arrival and we both went our separate ways. Two days later I gave her a call, and she said she was hoping I would call and that I would not stand her up.

We made a date that evening to go to Aruba's at the end of Commercial on Fort Lauderdale Beach. She gave me directions to her friend's house. When I got there, she was the only one home. She gave me a big kiss and hug as soon as she opened the door. I took her hand, walked her to the car, opened the door, and she got in. We put the top down and zoomed off to Aruba's for a romantic dinner looking out over the water. We had lobster and wine and dessert and hit it off in every way.

She was beautiful, had a great body, and was a well-put-together woman. She was very spiritual because she was a minister and I liked looking into her eyes. They were deep blue and she had a beautiful smile with perfect white teeth.

After dinner, we began to walk down the beach from Commercial Avenue to Oakland Park Boulevard. It was a star-filled night and she had a flowing white sundress on with a bikini under it. It was a warm night so she took her dress off and now she only had her bikini on with her sandals, the same sandals that had caught my eye when she was on the plane. Her body was fantastic and her being in a bikini really turned me on.

I was in shorts and a Tommy Bahamas shirt with dock sneakers on. As we walked in the sand, she took her sandals off and held them as she walked barefoot holding my hand. We got about halfway down the beach in a very dark area when she wanted to sit down. We sat down and listened to the waves and watched the water as it ebbed and flowed. Then we started making out. We kissed very deeply as we held hands and I could tell she knew how to kiss! Her lips were very sensual.

As we kissed, I could feel her nipples getting hard under her bikini top. She slipped her bikini top off and now she was topless while I kissed her nipples and caressed her breasts. She was getting very, very turned on. I put my hand in her bikini bottom and I could feel just how wet her pussy was. I began to stick my finger all the way up her vagina. She went crazy and started throwing sand up in the air, but it was a little odd because she didn't want to have sex; she only wanted to suck on my cock. With that, she began to lick the sides, then the tip, and take the whole thing in her mouth. She was moaning and groaning.

I could tell this was something she loved to do! All of a sudden she took her mouth off my dick and said, "I want you to cum in my mouth so I can taste and swallow the whole thing." She got so excited that I just couldn't control myself. When I came, I exploded in her mouth and she swallowed every last drop. I was completely dry, but she wanted more. She started sucking on me again, got me hard and I don't how she did it, but made me blow another gigantic load down her throat. She was completely insatiable.

After that round, we kissed, put our clothes back on and walked back to car. She said that she would call me at the end of the week and that she would like me to go with her back to Houston to meet her parents before she had to head back to Hawaii. I said I would think about it and then I dropped her off.

After that I went home and quite frankly didn't know what to think. I had never met a woman who liked swallowing cum so much. This was an incredible turn-on that I had never experienced to this degree before.

I spent the next couple of days working in the office on things, but could not get her out of my mind. I called her up and she agreed to drive over to my office that evening for an early dinner on 17th Street, before she had to fly back to Houston the next morning.

She arrived at my office and as soon as the door was closed, she began kissing me, and then dropped on her knees to suck me off again. This time not only did she suck me off, she took all of her clothes off and made me bend her over on my desk and make love to her the back way. She went crazy and then leapt up on the conference table so I could give it to her there. I did and then we went and had dinner. While we were eating, I decided that I would go to Houston a couple of days after she had gotten there.

I flew there two days later and she met me at the airport, embraced me, and we went to her parents' house. They lived in a very exclusive section of town in a mansion. Her father was a famous doctor and her mother was a socialite. They were friends with the Bushes and were very wealthy. I was to stay at their home in a separate bedroom that evening and then, formally meet them when we had dinner as soon as her father came home from the clinic that he owned.

Initially, when we got to her house, things were pretty tame until it was clear that we were alone. She was a little concerned that her mother might come home from her tennis lesson early, but that did not stop her from giving me a quickie in the living room where she could look out the window to see if anyone was coming into the driveway.

Shortly after we were done, her mother came home, so it was a close call. I met her mother and I could clearly see where she got her body and vivacious personality. Her mother was older, but a real hottie and I could tell she was doing more than playing tennis.

As soon as I met her father when he came home, my feelings were confirmed. While he was very successful, he was also an alcoholic. While still in his suit, we had to have drinks in the living room in order to get acquainted. Apparently, this was a formality that anyone who ever got involved with Helen had to go through. They had a maid that made and served all the drinks and after two drinks he was blasted.

He was fat and not very good looking so I had no doubt that the mother was whacking the tennis instructor or someone else. After the drinks we all went into the dining room and were served a gourmet dinner prepared by their private chef and served by the maid. This meal would stand up to one served in any five-star restaurant.

It was clear that these people were very affluent and had an excellent sense of social protocol. I had to watch my Ps and Qs and language while speaking to them.

By this time it was approximately nine PM and everyone was retiring. The father was hammered and was passing out at the dining room table. The mother left and went to the bedroom and closed the door.

I had a feeling that the father hadn't put his hands on her since the Regan administration. I could tell she was disgusted with his drinking and sloppy fat body and appearance. The father woke up and went into his office which was directly across the hall from my bedroom to supposedly do some work. I went to my room and said good night to Helen in a very formal manner—it was just good night and I will see you tomorrow. I put my pajamas on, shut the light off and got into bed.

I had laid there for about twenty minutes when I heard Helen speaking to her father in his office. At first they were talking quietly and then it got louder and I could hear her crying. The father began to berate her and tell her she was a loser because she was a minister and wasn't making any money. Then he said he was going to cut her off from the trust fund that her grandmother had left her until she got a real job.

Apparently Helen had asked for a monthly increase in whatever trust fund money she was receiving and her father had told her no. This arguing and crying went on for about half an hour, then she came out of the office and knocked on my bedroom door. I jumped up and opened the door and she came in.

She started hugging me and telling me what a bastard her father was and that he was very unfair to her because all of her other siblings were doctors and lawyers. She was the big disappointment in the family because she became a minister and of course, none of them could understand that.

Then she started kissing me and grabbing me and the next thing you know, she went down on me. She said it made her feel good to suck my dick and swallow my load. She told me it was comforting to her. It made her feel important and needed.

I wasn't going to question her motives because she was so good at this. I just let her do her thing. This went on for about an hour. Then she left my room and went to hers. The next morning, I was up early, got ready and she took me to the airport for my six AM flight back to Ft. Lauderdale. Thank God I did not run into Jane while waiting at the airport…

After I got back to Florida, Helen called me and invited me to come to Maui for my birthday. She said we would have a wonderful time and that she would introduce me to all of her longtime friends that lived on the island. She even said she would throw a big birthday party for me with a cake and all the trimmings. At first I wasn't so sure, but then I said why not?

Actually, the flight was the only thing that was bothering me. It was about a nine-hour flight to get there and I was tired of long, boring flights. After some thought, I decided to go and had Judy make the arrangements. I flew there first class so I would be as fresh and well rested as I could be when I touched down at Kahului airport.

The plane landed and there she was, waiting with a lei to put around my neck and welcome me Hawaiian style. She took me on a little tour of Maui and then we made our way to the little house she lived in with her roommate Carol. It was a beautiful open-air house with vaulted ceilings and a very special layout. That first night I was very tired, but after an early dinner, we proceeded to have some of the most intense oral sex that I had ever had! It seemed like we were making the sequel to *Deep Throat*. The next morning we got up and she took me to a great little breakfast place, off the beaten path, that nobody would ever know about.

The next evening she threw me a great birthday party that I must say was well planned. She invited all of her friends, none of whom I knew, but they made me feel very welcome and at home. She had a beautiful dinner catered and had a large birthday cake wheeled in. This was on a Saturday night and the party went on until about midnight.

The next morning we went to church with all the same people we had been with the night before. I began to understand how the people who actually live on the island can afford it. Most of them were either independently wealthy authors or had something going that generated them so much money they did not have to do anything except live on an island—which is exactly what they did. Not a financial worry in the world!

At the party it became clear that Helen had just broken up with a guy she had been dating for several years. That explained why she took me to an out-of-the-way breakfast place. She didn't want to run into him or he would see her with me.

The next few days were magical. We went on a helicopter ride over the waterfalls, then out to the continuous lava flow that goes into the ocean. We even stayed in an exclusive hotel on an island right off the coast of Maui. She dressed in sexy lingerie and treated me like royalty. She was like having my own personal sex goddess at my disposal. I stayed for five days and had a wonderful time. Then it was time to go back to Ft. Lauderdale and resume my cruising.

For a couple of weeks, I spoke to Jane on and off, but I could tell she wasn't for me. Helen and I talked every day and then, out of the blue, Helen said she wanted to move back to Ft. Lauderdale. She said she was getting island fever from being on Maui too long and needed to get back on the mainland.

I had a beautiful house in Weston Hills that was vacant, so this was the perfect opportunity to bring Helen to Ft. Lauderdale and have her stay in my house while she decided what she wanted to do. Initially, she was going to try and get into a local church where she thought she might have a shot at being a minister. Okay, here we go again…

CHAPTER 19

It was the week between Christmas and New Year's of 1999. Helen was all set to fly back to Fort Lauderdale after the first week of January 2000. Before that she invited me to go with her to her parents' ski lodge in Breckenridge, Colorado, to do some skiing, snowboarding, and spend time with her family. I accepted the invitation and right after Christmas with my family, I left to go to Colorado.

I flew to Denver and she picked me up and we drove on I-70 to Breckenridge. Her parents had a condominium right on the slopes and not too far from downtown. I met them again and we all had dinner on Main Street in a restaurant with a roaring fireplace. I met her entire family, her parents, her brothers and sisters, their spouses, and all the kids. We had a wonderful time for three days and then Helen and I decided to leave on New Year's Eve morning and fly back through Las Vegas so we could see the fireworks shoot off from all the hotels.

We took off from Denver and landed in Las Vegas at about nine o'clock on New Year's Eve. We checked into the Flamingo Hotel, made love, and then went out onto the Strip to get ready for the show. We stood there in the sea of people on Las Vegas Boulevard, and at the stroke of midnight, the fireworks went off from eight hotels. That was truly a sight to see. We were both mesmerized by the pyrotechnics. The thirty-minute display seemed to go on forever.

When that ended, we went back to the room, had a glass of wine and toasted the New Year again. After all it was the turn of the century—an extra special New Year's Eve for sure! We made love again and this time she said she had to swallow my load, which she did. Jesus, this woman was obsessed with eating cum so much that I nicknamed her the "Gulper."

The next morning, we took separate flights back to where we had come from. She took a flight back to Hawaii to gather up her things and get ready to permanently relocate in Fort Lauderdale and I took a flight back to Fort Lauderdale to get things ready at the house for her arrival. Everything seemed to be going very well. She and I got along famously.

Once she and her dog flew in from Hawaii and got to my house, she organized everything, and it seemed like we were going to be a couple. She was clean and neat and had everything in place, plus she always looked very nice and well put together. At a moment's notice, she would take her top off, get on her knees, and give me a blowjob or take all of her clothes off and want to have wild sex. She always used a small vibrator while I was inside her. This seemed to give her a double thrill.

She made me have sex with her in the bathroom, the kitchen, living room and every evening after dinner she made me sit on the couch, pulled my pants down, told me to relax and gave me a slow, long, deep, blowjob while she still had her kitchen apron on. She made me gourmet dinners then sucked on me until I blew my load. Then, she would say it was time to go to sleep. What more could a man ask for?

Initially while I was with her, I was going back and forth to my family's house in Davie, staying for one or two days, and then telling Kristen I had to go on a cruise. Meanwhile I would go back to Weston and stay with Helen. Sometimes I really would go on a cruise and be gone for four or five days and then come back and juggle going to both places. This was a real challenge, but I always seemed to be able to pull it off.

About the third week of January, Holland America sent me on a cruise that took me to St. Thomas to do training on several ships as they came in. While I was doing training on one of the ships, I got a phone call from Judy, my secretary, telling me that Helen had been spotted driving in my Mercedes around town with another guy in the passenger seat. That being bad enough, she also told me that she was spotted by a captain friend of mine in the parking lot of a Thai restaurant on Sunrise Boulevard making love to him in the front seat of my car. She gave me the guy's number and told me to call him right away.

I did and did I get an earful. He told me it was definitely my car, and because he had met her, he made a positive identification so I knew he wasn't making it up. He even described the guy and I knew that this was one of Helen's old acquaintances. Once I got off the phone with him, I called Helen and I asked her where she had been that evening.

She lied, of course, and when I confronted her with the truth, she immediately hung up on me. I tried to call her back, but she didn't answer. I was scheduled to go back to Fort Lauderdale the next day and when I got to the house all her things were gone and the car was parked in the garage. Everything was like she had never been there.

I immediately got in my car and went down to Fort Lauderdale to see if I could find her at her friend's house or the church that she attended. I actually did find her at her friend's house and asked her to explain what was going on. When I got her outside, she began to cry and told me that she had had feelings for this guy for a long time and that she didn't think it would work out with her and me.

This was just after I had moved her and got her settled. Now she was leaving and moving in with him. So that was the end of Helen. She was gone. What could I say? I only knew one thing; I would sure miss getting those unbelievable blowjobs. She asked me to stay in touch with her, but I decided not to. Now, I was back to square one. She is still a minister to this day and she actually married the guy.

I went back to the condominium that Kristen and I had and decided to lay low for a while. That didn't last for long. Norwegian Cruise Lines set me up on another eight cruises starting out with going on the *Norway* out of Miami. I had to train about eight hundred people, so I went to the office and had Judy prepare the training manuals as I got ready for my trip which was to take place the following Saturday.

As usual I went down to the dock, got all my stuff loaded on the ship, and then embarked as a contractor and got my cabin assigned to me. The *Norway* was one of the last great oceangoing vessels with its very long promenade decks on each side. The ship was also as long as the Statue of Liberty was high, one of the largest ships still sailing on the seas.

The first day out was pretty uneventful. We left Miami at five in the afternoon and sailed out through the Intracoastal Waterway toward the Gulf of Mexico, heading toward the Caribbean. This itinerary would take us to St. Thomas, St. Maarten, St. Kitts, and then back again. It was a full seven-day cruise.

All of the cruises to the eastern Caribbean were spectacular. They were filled with beautiful scenery, gorgeous sunsets, and a true feeling of the island paradise. St. Maarten was my favorite and the beaches there were beyond compare, especially on the French side of the island.

On the second day out, right before we landed in St. Maarten, while sitting in the lounge, I met four girls who were sitting together because they all went on vacation as a reunion of sorts. One of them lived in Delray Beach, Florida. Her name was Gloria, and she was a little older than the others, but, boy, was she good-looking!

She had a beautiful, heart-shaped face, and a voluptuous body. Her eyes were piercing green and her hair was blonde. She was a little taller than me, but she seemed to like me very much. We sat and chatted and had a couple of drinks. She was very prim and proper and very much a lady—at least that was what I thought. We chatted in the lounge for a few hours after dinner and then we adjourned for the night and went to our own cabins. We had made plans to go ashore on St. Maarten the next day since I didn't have any training classes scheduled until we were out at sea again.

I was up early the next morning and was looking forward to seeing Gloria down by the gangway where we were to meet. I was in my civilian attire—shorts, Hawaiian shirt, and boat sneakers. When I saw her coming, she looked like a movie star! She had gorgeous white pants on, sandals with her beautiful toes showing, a frilly top, a big sun hat, glasses, and hoop earrings. She had bright red lipstick on which made her even more desirable. Her toes were red, her nails were red, and her lips were red. Boy, did I like red!

We embraced and said good morning and then held hands as we went down the gangway onto the landing craft. The boat filled up and we were off to the dock on St. Maarten. As soon as we disembarked, we began to walk and look at all the shops and jewelry stores. After an hour of that, we decided to go to the front side of the island. Anybody that's ever been to St. Maarten knows that the front side of the island is much nicer and the beaches are just gorgeous. You can go to the beach, get served incredible drinks and food, all while you're lying on your lounge chair. It is truly a tropical paradise. The water is warm enough to walk right in and not get a chill. That is the way I like it!

As soon as we got to the beach, Gloria took off her pants and top and she had on a tiny bikini. Because it was a topless beach, she took her top off. She had beautiful breasts and perky nipples and her body looked perfect with just a little bikini bottom on. Keep in mind this was a woman in her early fifties. She looked ravishing!

I tried not to stare at her breasts too much or make a big deal out of it, but as I lay down next to her on a chaise lounge, I couldn't help being aroused. I was getting a hard-on just thinking about being next to her. To distract myself, I went in the water, ordered food, went on a walk— did anything I could just so I wouldn't be thinking about wanting to get her in bed.

I did pretty well because we managed to get through the whole afternoon and I acted like a gentleman, although I had every dirty thought in my mind about her and what I wanted to do to her when I got her alone. It was a hot sunny afternoon and even with sunscreen, her boobs got sunburned and they were very sensitive. Before I knew it, it was four o'clock and we had to catch a taxi back to the dock to be picked up by the landing craft and brought back to the ship for the six o'clock departure.

We made it back and decided to meet for dinner after we had a chance to shower and change. I met her in the main dining room. She looked suntanned and a little red, but stunningly beautiful. She also smelled incredible with her fresh hair and delicious perfume.

Only two of her friends joined us and they decided to leave early, leaving us by ourselves. We chatted for a little while, then went out on the deck for a walk. We began to kiss. She was a scrumptious kisser and seemed to always hold my hand and squeeze it while I was kissing her. It was very tame for the most part. We made a date to see each other when we got back to Miami. She was very polite, gave me her number, and said for me to please call her the following week. The next day I had intense training classes and did not see her that evening. The ship docked back in Miami early that morning.

I disembarked by way of the crew gangway and did not see Gloria. It was a Saturday and I headed directly back to the office to print out my training certificates. I had Gloria's number and my plan was to call the following Monday in order for us to make a date for dinner during the week.

I held out until Tuesday to call her. She didn't answer so I left a message. This was her home so I waited until the following evening to call her. Finally, she answered the phone and sounded glad that I had called and accepted a date to go with me on my boat the following Saturday down the Intracoastal Waterway to have lunch somewhere in Miami.

Saturday morning came and I picked her up at her house in Delray Beach. We drove back down to Fort Lauderdale to where my boat was docked on the Intracoastal Waterway right in downtown Fort Lauderdale. When my yacht came into sight, she was visibly impressed and interested to see what it was like. We boarded the yacht, took all the covers off, and got everything ready to head out for the day.

She looked great again in shorts and a little top. She was wearing boat sneakers and her hair was up in a ponytail. Again, for a fifty-year-old woman she was gorgeous! She looked a little like Doris Day.

We untied the boat and took off. She was impressed with my captaining skills as we made our way south on the Intracoastal. She sat up on the bridge with me as I maneuvered through the Waterway and called for the various bridge openings on the way down. We decided to stop at a restaurant in North Miami. I docked the boat smoothly, tied it up, and we went in. It was magical. We sat there on a gorgeous summer afternoon looking out at my yacht and having a great lunch as the seagulls landed on the pilings by the dock. As soon as we finished, we got back on the boat and headed all the way down to the port of Miami so we could dock and then walk around before we had to return.

It was getting a little late in the afternoon and I did not like to drive at night so we only had about an hour and a half in Miami to look around, then get back on the boat, head out to the ocean, and then straight north back to the Port Everglades and inlet. It was much faster going back if you came up on the ocean side instead of going all the way up the Intracoastal at no-wake speed.

Once we got a mile from shore, I pushed the throttle up. We were going about twenty knots—fast for a fifty-foot yacht. It was a calm sea with a very light chop, so it was pretty smooth. As we got closer to Fort Lauderdale, I slowed it down a bit so we could spend a little time out in the ocean. We started to kiss each other in our bathing suits while we were up on the bridge. We were kissing passionately and I pushed her head down so she could suck my dick.

She resisted, and then said that she would do it, but this was not her favorite thing. She said she'd had a bad experience with someone who had forced her to go down on him all the time and swallow his loads, so this was something she hated. I didn't know what to say.

Reluctantly she gave me a blowjob, but it wasn't very good. It was only marginal, but she did it, and then she came back up and started kissing me again. Right before we went to the inlet, she asked me if I would pull her bikini bottoms down and lick her pussy. I said of course.

She took her bottoms down and I put my tongue right in her crack. At that moment, she rolled her eyes back in her head and lay down right on the cushion and let me lick her till she came. She was screaming her head off and told me she loved to be eaten out. This drove her out of her mind. She got so insane that she couldn't even talk and she would start to shake and when she came, she lost total control and would also start to pee, so I better watch out!

I licked her for about five minutes and she exploded. I wasn't sure if she was squirting juice or pee—all I know is she had a giant orgasm and in fact she had two or three during the same session. I could see why this was her favorite thing. After that, she wanted me to stick my dick inside of her as she then proceeded to fuck the shit out of me.

She grabbed onto my penis and just humped me until the cows came home. She loved to screw and get her pussy eaten out. These were her hot buttons! She definitely was sex-crazed!

We got back to the dock and kissed again passionately. Then she wanted me to touch her again, which I did. Then she asked me to take her home. When we got to her house, she took me by the hand, brought me upstairs, took a shower with me, and wanted me to eat her pussy out again. I did and that was the most erotic shower I had ever had.

This time she got down on her knees in the shower and sucked my dick. Then she insisted that I lick her while she was standing up as I pinched both of her nipples at the same time. I had a wild one on my hands for sure!

After we were done I cleaned up again and went home. Because Gloria lived so close, I knew I had to get another place. The Weston house was going to be sold and going there would not be an option anymore, so I decided to rent a penthouse apartment on the Intracoastal up on the sixteenth floor of a beautiful new complex being built called Sunrise Towers. It was almost completed, and I went down there and looked at this gorgeous two-bedroom apartment with a balcony that overlooked the Intracoastal and the ocean. I took it and began to get the place ready to be my new hideout.

I signed the lease and was ready to move in by June of 2000. I was seeing Gloria during this time, always going to her house to pick her up, go out to eat, and taking her back to her house to make love to her and eat her out. This is what we did week after week and month after month. She worked so she didn't mind staying close to her home in Delray Beach because she had to be up early the next morning.

I actually told her I lived on the boat. I had clothing there and everything else, and it seemed as if you could live on the boat. It was surely big enough. She didn't question it and loved to go out with me on it so we could be free. Whenever we did go out on the boat, as soon as we got past where anybody could see us, she would take her bathing suit off and be completely naked. She was really something! When she was naked I couldn't resist getting a full erection—as she saw that, she knew what was coming next and, boy, did she want it!

The first of May, I got the keys to the new apartment and immediately began to decorate it. I had the walls painted and went out and got designer furniture and fixtures to make the place look like a model home. From bedding to glasses to towels, everything was perfect. I even had big-screen TVs put in each of the bedrooms inside hand-built cabinets. The place was spectacular—right down to the furniture on the balcony. Now I had a great place to bring Gloria or anybody else!

CHAPTER 20

Gloria loved my apartment. She couldn't wait to bring some of her clothes there, including boating outfits so she could be near the beach and the boat. The apartment came with a boat slip. I parked my yacht so I could see it when looking down from the balcony. When I was out of town, Gloria would go there and spend the weekends just relaxing, lying on the balcony, or going up to the pool deck that was on the roof of the complex. They had a beautiful restaurant and bar that served tropical drinks and finger food all day long.

It was now summer and I was getting ready to go on another cruise for Holland America. This time it was to St. Thomas and then back through Puerto Rico to Miami. I was always allowed to bring someone with me and I asked Gloria if she wanted to go. She said yes, of course, and prepared to leave with me the following weekend.

Gloria worked at a company in Miami so she arranged to take seven days off with me so we could cruise. That next Saturday morning, we left from my apartment, went to Fort Lauderdale airport, and flew all the way to St. Thomas where we picked up the ship as it set sail back to Puerto Rico. We arrived in St. Thomas early in the day and rented a Jeep so we could drive around the island, go have lunch at the Marriott Hotel up on the hill, and then board the ship before five PM when I left.

Once on board we got assigned our cabin and, as usual, it was gorgeous with a balcony. The weather was beautiful and Gloria could not wait to take her clothes off and lie on the balcony overlooking the ocean when we were out at sea. That evening we made love on the balcony. We could hear the waves breaking against the bow as the ship made its way to Puerto Rico.

The next morning, I had a training class so I left Gloria to do whatever she wanted to do while I did my job. That evening we had dinner on the Lido deck together, then went back to the cabin. She insisted that I go down on her, which as you know was her favorite thing. This time when I was eating her, she got so insane that she grabbed the radio on the nightstand and threw it against the wall and started biting on the pillow. She absolutely went wild! She was out of breath and out of control and started to hyperventilate—so much so that I had to stop so she could calm down and regain her composure. She came so many times that I thought she was going to have a heart attack! I had never been with a woman who was so insatiable!

It was a two-day trip back to Puerto Rico. Once we docked, Gloria and I disembarked at Old Town and walked in and out of all the shops and down to the Fort. Then we took a taxi to the Hilton on the other side of the island where Holland America put us up for the evening at their expense while I waited for another ship to come in the next morning that would take us back to Fort Lauderdale.

When we checked into the hotel, they had no rooms left except for the special suite that was reserved for celebrities. Sylvester Stallone was the one that always got the room that they gave us. It was literally two stories with a living room and dining room, three bedrooms, and three full bathrooms. It had a spacious living room that had a panoramic view of the ocean and was just out of this world.

When we got to the room, Gloria fell on the bed, grabbed me, and wanted me to bang the hell out of her—which is exactly what I did.

Then she made me go down on her again and this time her pussy was squirting like a water pistol! She went insane!

After we were done, we got dressed and walked next door to Morton's Steakhouse for dinner. After dinner, we walked all over the complex, through the garden, and then down to the ocean to watch the sunset. She took her shoes off and walked in the sand while the sun went down. She had seen a beautiful dress in the window of one of the shops and we went in and I bought it for her. She was truly a girly girl and, although she was wild in bed, she was very much a lady when we were out in public. This really turned me on because I knew what I was in for as soon as we got behind closed doors.

At dinner we had had some wine and she was a little looped. When we got into the room, she immediately stripped, took a shower, and then came right after me. She was bending over the bathroom sink while she was washing her face and told me to give it to her while she was bent over. She went wild and was hanging onto the faucets for dear life as her thighs quivered and she almost went into a coma while we made love.

Because she was so vocal, it made me get harder and harder, and that made me bang her even better. This went on until she couldn't take it anymore and I literally had to carry her back to the bed where she fell asleep hanging onto me for dear life.

The next day the *Volendamm* pulled into port and we made our way back to Old Town and boarded the ship for the return trip to Miami. I had to do several training classes on that ship as well, but my work didn't keep us from having a wonderful time.

When we got back to Miami, I drove her back to Deerfield Beach and I went home. The next day, she had to go to work and I had to do some work at the office and prepare for another cruise, so we couldn't see each other for a couple of days. About Wednesday of that week, I called her and we made a date to have dinner. I said I would be there at six o'clock and she said fine, the door would be open, and I should just come upstairs when I got to her place.

I arrived at her condo, opened the door, and didn't hear a thing. I looked around and then I heard her say, "I'm upstairs—come get me."

As I went up the stairs I could smell scented candles. I walked into the bedroom and found the entire place had candles glowing, with her lying on the bed in a negligee with no panties. The room was dark other than the glow of the candles—there must have been at least thirty of them lit up. There was just enough light so I could see what I was doing—and believe me, I knew what she wanted me to do.

As soon as I saw this, I took all my clothes off slowly, went down on her, and watched her go insane again as I licked every crevice of her vagina. Again she went wild and came multiple times while screaming! This woman was totally out of control when it came to having her pussy licked. She was completely insatiable! One time when I was eating her out, she went so crazy she grabbed the VCR next to the bed and threw it against the wall, smashing it into a million pieces. It scared the hell out of me!

It was now the middle of the summer and we continued to see each other at least several times a week. On weekends we would go on my boat when I wasn't going on a cruise. Suddenly, for whatever reason, I received phone calls from Tamara, Helen, and Maria all in the same week. They all said they missed me and wanted to get together again. Oh my God, now what would I do?

This all came out of left field and the way I was, I just couldn't pass the opportunity up. At the same time, because the apartment complex was new, the leasing agent wanted to introduce me to a newly single woman who lived on the sixth floor named Bebe.

While I was in the leasing office paying the rent, the agent called Bebe and summoned her to the office. She came in and my eyes lit up—another hot number who was recently divorced. Bebe was vivacious, with a beautiful body and big boobies that I knew were artificial, but she had a great personality, a gorgeous smile, and seemed eager to meet someone. We made a date for lunch for sometime the following week.

I was in a little bit of a dry spell from having to go on cruises, so I was around town, going to Shooters on the Intracoastal and the Bimini boatyard on 17th Street. Now that I had this apartment I could bring anybody I wanted to up there with ease.

Because all of these women had suddenly come out of the woodwork, I felt I had to change my identity so no one would know—at least at the gatehouse. I also did not want any of the women knowing who was visiting me before them. I contacted the guards on all the shifts that let people in and out of the complex, paid them off, and now my new name was "Tony Bosimotto." All the guards had my cell phone number and they would alert me if anyone came to the complex while I was there with someone else. They would not allow them in if that was the case.

Now I was seeing Gloria, but had invited Helen up because she had called me and said she was sorry about how everything ended and that she missed me. Then Tamara showed up and Maria surfaced again. In addition, I started to take Bebe out to lunch and even sometimes dinner on a regular basis.

One unforgettable Saturday, Gloria came over in the morning and we had wild sex, then Tamara came over and I gave it to her, then Maria showed up. I did her and then that evening I went out to dinner with Bebe! Can you imagine? There was a front and back elevator in the building so I had one coming up the front elevator, while one was leaving on the back elevator. This was totally insane, but oh my God, what a thrill!

Believe it or not, I never had sex with Bebe. I only kissed her hello on the cheek and then kissed her goodbye after our dinners and took her to some very nice places that were pretty pricey. I could tell that she had the eye for guys with money, a lot more money than me. She was newly divorced, but she was a realtor and she managed to get a job in a high-rise condo on the Intracoastal Waterway near Fort Lauderdale. It was a pretty swanky place and she immediately got close to the guy that put up the building. His name was Jon and he was from South Africa.

While I continued to take her to lunch, I noticed that anytime I asked her to go to dinner she had plans so I put a private detective on her. It didn't take long to see that she was going out with this guy and they were becoming an item. She was all over Fort Lauderdale with him at all the most expensive restaurants and nightclubs around town. They were always together, and the next thing you know she didn't want to see me anymore because they had moved into a beach house right across from Fort Lauderdale Beach.

Apparently, this guy came from Tampa where he had a family and several kids. He got involved with this project in Fort Lauderdale and then he got involved with Bebe. The long and short of it is, he left his wife, they got a divorce, and he and Bebe began living together. They got engaged and planned to be married over Christmas.

I backed off when I found out what was going on and rightly so because I could see there was no future with her. I continued to see Gloria as well as the other girls on and off and then sometimes on a regular basis, but around the holiday time I usually stayed close to my own family—at least for a little while.

Bebe and Jon got married the day before Christmas Eve of 2000. On Christmas Eve, Jon was on the I-95, driving north and had a massive heart attack in the car. He died on the spot one day after they were married. Needless to say, Bebe was devastated and her entire world was shattered after all they had gone through to be together.

I attended the funeral and it was clear Bebe would never be the same again. In later years I found out she had met another married guy who was a contractor and the whole thing repeated itself, except this time the guy didn't die—although he went broke buying her cars, jewelry, and homes. She was something and to my knowledge she's still hanging around Fort Lauderdale somewhere, but I have no idea who she's with or what she's up to.

On Christmas Day 2000, Gloria suddenly called me and told me she wanted me to come to visit her for Christmas at her condo. If I didn't come, she was going to break up with me. I didn't know what was going on, but concocted an elaborate scheme to meet her demand. I had the chief compliance officer of Carnival Cruise Lines call my house while I was at Christmas dinner and tell me that I had to go to Port Canaveral for a hazardous waste emergency. He did, and I left and then went to Gloria's.

When I got there, she had a full-blown Christmas party going on, and her only issue was that she wanted me to be there. I stayed for a while and just as I was going to leave, everyone else left and then she took me upstairs and whacked the hell out of me again. I didn't get home until eleven that night. Everyone was asleep, but they thought I had a work issue, so nobody gave me any grief.

With the turn of the New Year, juggling all these women was starting to get old. It seemed like it was a constant cycle that I couldn't break and I didn't know what to do. In spite of the fact that I had had a heart attack, my libido was always in overdrive.

The Weston house was sold and Kristen and I began living in a condo in Davie. I still had the apartment on the Intracoastal. The yacht was parked there. Kristen didn't know about the yacht until two years later. The cruise lines continued to send me on cruises all over the world and I continued to meet women, one after another. At one point during that year, I was seeing eleven women at the same time! Some of them were from Florida, but many of them were from all over the country.

In February of 2001, I went to a local trade show in Boca Raton, where I was displaying the machine that I had invented several years before. The machine ground up florescent light bulbs, extracted the mercury, and then collected the glass. It was truly revolutionary and I even got a patent on it.

While I was at this trade show, a gorgeous redhead walked up to my booth, looked at me and said that I was very handsome and what would she have to do to have lunch with me? Oh God, here we go again... and what a come-on!

I'd never been with a redhead before and Judy was very pretty and Irish-looking with a great smile, high cheekbones, and very well-built. We made a date to go have lunch at Mangoes on Las Olas in Fort Lauderdale.

We met for lunch the next day and after two cosmopolitans, she told me she wanted to have sex with me. I was never one to turn down an invitation like that, so I took her back to the apartment. Once we got there she ripped all of her clothes off and literally attacked me. She gave me a blowjob, but more importantly, she just wanted me to stick it in her and keep giving it to her. All she kept saying was "Don't stop, don't stop." Frankly, I couldn't keep up with her. She was bucking and holding onto her toes while she kept screaming "Don't stop." I couldn't hold it anymore. I blew my load and then she finally calmed down a little after I continued by using my fingers.

She was so wet that she made a mess of all the sheets and blankets. Oh well, that's what washing machines are for.

Her husband was an airline pilot who lived in Singapore. He was based there for three months at a time and came home for two weeks after that and then went back. She was alone a lot, played a lot of tennis, did her job as an insurance agent, but wanted somebody just to have sex with. I was it!

At least twice a week when I was in town, I would go to her condo in the morning. She would make bacon and eggs and toast, we would talk and then go to the bedroom where she would take all of her clothes off and give me great head. We would make love while her bulldog Otis watched. When we were through, she would wash me off, I would get dressed, she would kiss me goodbye and I would go back to my office. There were no strings attached, and when her husband was in town I didn't hear from her until he went back to Asia. This was a perfect setup. I never even had to take her to dinner—or lunch for that matter. All she wanted was a good whacking and I gave it to her.

This went on for several months without any complications. I was still seeing Gloria from time to time, but that was fading as well and Tamara had only come back to see me because she had broken up with her new boyfriend for a brief time, but then she got back together with him.

Maria was living in Miami and wanted to get back together with me because we had been together so many years earlier, but I could tell that was never going to work out with her overbearing Peruvian personality. She liked to control everything and I was not one to be controlled.

During this time, Jane from Texas called me again and came to Fort Lauderdale once more to visit me. I took her to my apartment and she went crazy, telling me how beautiful it was and how much she loved me and, of course, that she also wanted to move to Fort Lauderdale, but that never happened.

I continued to go on cruises into the spring of 2001 and continued to meet women, many of them, on every cruise. It was truly out of control. Luckily most of the ones I met didn't live in Fort Lauderdale, so I didn't have to contend with anyone on a daily basis.

On one Royal Caribbean cruise, I was attending a show when I felt a tap on my shoulder. It was an older lady sitting behind me. She had overheard me speaking to someone when I said I lived in Fort Lauderdale. She said she would be in Miami and when I turned around she introduced me to her husband, a Dade County appellate court judge.

When the show ended, we all walked out of the theater together, but she stayed behind so she could walk next to me. Her husband was in front of us and he told her that he was tired and he was going back to the cabin. She invited me to have a drink with her at the bar.

We went to the bar and she began to knock down drinks and tell me just how much she wanted to have an affair while she was on the ship. She asked for my cabin number just as I was telling her I was turning in for the night. I had a training class the next day so I had to be on my best game. She wasn't bad looking for an older woman—probably at least sixty to my forty-nine.

I gave her my cabin number and I left. I went back to my cabin, put my pajamas on, and went to sleep. About an hour later, I heard a knock at my door, which startled me. I jumped up and opened it to see who it was.

It was her and she had a bottle of wine. Her shoes were off and she stuck her leg in the cabin and pulled herself right into the middle of the room and immediately took all of her clothes off. She told me she wanted me to fuck the hell out of her because she hadn't had any in several years! Wow! Another sex maniac!

She literally attacked me. She sucked on me, grabbed my dick, made me kiss her nipples and pull her hair, anything and everything to get her excited. When I started to lick her pussy, she began squirming and bouncing all over the bed. I had to hold her down with all my strength or she would have broken my nose! Apparently, no one had ever done that to her before. This was a whole new thing and, boy, did she like it!

This went on for several hours and then I finally told her she had to leave—I needed to get some sleep. She gave me her phone number, and told me to call her when I got back to Miami. I didn't see her for the rest of the trip. I guess we got off the ship and missed each other. But I was looking forward to calling her the following week.

I called her on Tuesday and she said she had been waiting for my call and couldn't wait to see me again. She asked me where my office was, and she was there at noon in a new Jaguar. She picked me up, took me down to Hollywood Beach for lunch, and then took me to a hotel in Hollywood and told me that she wanted to make love with me for two hours while she had the time.

She was very wealthy and it was clear all she wanted was an affair that she could count on every week or two. Her husband, who was older than she was, was impotent and she yearned for some younger cock—actually, any cock—and I was the lucky candidate!

One day she came to my office when I was there on a Saturday morning doing some work for the next cruise. She took off all of her clothes, locked the door, made me lick her on the conference table and then sat on the copy machine and pushed the button so we could get copies of her ass. She thought this way I wouldn't forget about her. She was a little nutty, but fun nevertheless.

This was getting to be a love affair and I could tell that I had to cut this one off pretty soon. I had no desire to get involved with a powerful, rich woman whose husband was a judge. That was all I needed!

Gradually, I didn't take her calls anymore and then when I finally did, she told me she had met another guy who was closer to her age that wanted to marry her and lived in Miami. I heard she divorced her judge husband and the two of them ran off to Connecticut and got married. Apparently, that's what she wanted and that's what she got, but I was glad I was off the hook.

I had no shortage of crazy situations that occupied my time when

I was in Fort Lauderdale. With the apartment and the yacht, I always had someplace to go with someone and a place to hide out. Kristen was working at the police department and didn't seem interested in whether I was there or not. In hindsight, I can't say that I blame her. I'm sure in her heart she knew about everything but had gotten used to it and did not want to "rock the boat."

CHAPTER 21

Royal Caribbean, Carnival, and Holland America had scheduled me to sail on over twenty cruises in a two-month period. This was an insane schedule, but it took me to several ports I hadn't been to before. This time, I went to Bermuda, Turkey, and back and forth through the Panama Canal fifteen times.

The cruises were spectacular and I met several more beautiful women from everywhere and all walks of life. I had short-lived, but exciting romantic adventures with each one of them as we were able to disembark the ship and explore these new places together. Several were models, a few were European and some were from the Far East. They were exciting, mysterious, and erotic in their own way.

It seemed that none of them were interested in a long-term relationship. They only wanted to have fun while we are on the cruise. In most cases, after the cruise ended, I didn't see or talk to them again. Just as well, I needed a break from all of it.

One in particular was outstanding, however. Her name was Genette. She was a model and actress from Boca Raton, Florida. During the 1960s, she had been one of the girls that appeared with Jackie Gleason on television every week. She had the classic model's face with high cheekbones, beautiful green eyes, and voluptuous lips, and an incredible body. She was sensuous without doing anything.

When I met her on the ship, she was wearing dark sunglasses

and a big sun hat. She had a bikini on covered by a wrap that you could see through while she was lying on a chaise lounge. We hit it off immediately and I could tell she liked me as much as I liked her.

She really did look like an actress and many of the crew members and passengers were looking at both of us as we chatted on the deck. She never took her sunglasses off.

It just so happened I was staying in the presidential suite, the same suite where George Bush 41 stayed when he was on the ship. The suite was lavish and had panoramic views of the ocean, a full bar, gigantic bedroom, kitchen, living room, dining room, two giant bathrooms with full showers, and a wraparound balcony. Can you imagine—I was in this cabin all by myself? It was right below the captain's quarters, which were just as lavish.

Genette and I had dinner that evening and I asked her if she would like to come back to see the presidential suite. She, of course, said yes. She was amazed at how big it was and how beautiful all the decorations were. We sat on the sumptuous couch and began to have wine. There was a full wine bar in the cabin with many expensive French wines—all on the house.

After several minutes, we began to tongue kiss and I gradually began to take her clothes off. At first she resisted, but then she started to help me. We both undressed and I dimmed all the lights in the cabin as she looked over the open ocean on the moonlit night.

Her specialty was slowly giving me incredible hand jobs. While she began to do this and softly stroke my penis, she began talking about the male anatomy and just how special it was. While she softly touched me, she began to lick her lips and told me that she wanted to suck on me. She actually asked me for permission to go down on me. This made it even more exciting!

She gave me an incredible blowjob and then lay on the couch and opened her legs up as wide as she could and asked me to make love to her. She moaned and groaned and screamed and then came. When she came, she quivered and then went limp. She was very special and a real sensual being.

We stayed together on the cruise until we got back to Miami. I took her number, called the following week, and went up to Boca to see her.

She lived in an apartment and worked as a receptionist at the Fort Lauderdale Art Institute. She had been given the cruise as a gift by her ex-husband and was now beginning to live life again as a single woman. Her ex-husband was very wealthy and took care of everything for her, so for her to be on her own was something new that she hadn't experienced for a long time.

As soon as I got to her apartment, I could see that she was very disorganized, and didn't know how to take care of anything because she had always had a maid and didn't know how to manage money at all. She didn't even know how to balance a checkbook or cook. This was a woman who had been taken care of by men her whole life. First by her husband with whom she had her children and then by several husbands who fell for her beauty as hard as I did.

She was a real handful. She liked to sleep, could barely get up for work, and had a car that her ex-husband had given her that was in need of some work because she didn't know a thing about cars. She was pretty much flying by the seat of her pants.

Every morning she would drive from Boca down to Fort Lauderdale and I would meet her for breakfast at the 17th Street Diner. We would have coffee, talk, and hold hands and then she would go to work. After work I would meet her for dinner and we would go someplace near the art school to grab a bite to eat.

This was okay for a while and I could quickly see that this was what it was going to be. She had no ability to take care of anything because she was so used to being taken care of. One day when we were leaving the diner, she grabbed the handle to open the car door and the handle fell off. This made her cry and she was absolutely confused as to what to do.

She was quickly running out of the money that her ex-husband had given her as part of the divorce settlement and now it was clear that she needed someone new or she was completely going to fall apart. For a short time, it seemed like it was going to be me.

For several weeks when I was in town, we would meet at various hotels up and down the I-95 between Boca and Fort Lauderdale. We would spend several hours or sometimes the night making love, talking, and having dinner, but she didn't have anything to offer other than that. I actually felt sorry for her because her car had quit on her. I leased a brand-new Honda Accord for her.

I picked up the car at Hollywood Honda and brought it over to my office. I asked her to come to my office on a Saturday and told her the car was hers and gave her the keys. She started crying and said "Oh thank you, John, thank you," and began to make love to me right in my office.

She had almost lost her job several times because she couldn't make it to work because her car had broken down. After she left my office, she took off in the new car and had the rental company pick the rental up at my office. That was that.

She had a leased car that I was paying for. In exchange for that, she would meet me for breakfast or dinner, make love to me, and then we both go about our business. I was on cruises and I only saw her maybe once or twice every two weeks and the meetings and the conversations and the lovemaking were getting old.

One day when I was at my office, she called me in tears and told me she had been fired. She was extremely disorganized and apparently did not relay specific messages to the correct people at the art school and this had resulted in her dismissal. Now she had no job and was still riding around in my car. I had to give her a gas credit card and help her pay for her apartment because the rent was due the following week. I almost had no choice.

Initially she went looking for jobs, but nobody would hire her because she didn't have a marketable skill set other than the fact that she was nice to look at and relatively articulate. She had very limited computer skills and, as I mentioned, she was not organized at all. According to her, several of her interviews were about the owner of the company latching onto her because she was so beautiful and had a sensual allure. She said she wanted no part of that and only wanted the job that would pay her enough that she could support herself.

After several weeks of looking for a job, she became very despondent. Once when I was at her apartment during that time, she wanted me to make her pregnant. With that I jumped up and said no way! She just wanted to lock onto me with the child, so I would be hooked to her for the rest of her life. I knew right then and there I had to get out and get out fast!

I told her that we had to end the relationship, but she could still drive the car and as soon as she got a job she could begin paying for it or at least pay for the gas. She agreed and then she left. I went on several cruises and when I got back I didn't hear from her, but of course the bill from the leasing company came in and I paid. About a month went by and suddenly I got a call from her down in Key West, Florida. She had run out of gas, and the car was stuck in Key West and so was she.

Apparently, she had hooked up with another guy. They went down to Key West, had a good time, and the next thing you know he was gone. She had no money, the car was out of gas, and she was stuck.

I drove down there, retrieved her and the car, and brought them back to Fort Lauderdale. During this time, she lost her apartment and was staying with a friend. She was a total wreck and didn't look very good because she couldn't afford to buy makeup. The car was a mess and had cigarette burns all over the interior. The guy she had been with was a smoker and was a real slob.

Because I had feelings for her, I gave her $2000 to get herself back on her feet and she managed to get a job as a receptionist in a real estate company. I thought at least for a while she was going to be okay. I took off again on a cruise and then didn't hear from her for several weeks. Then I got a phone call from the police that they had found my car badly damaged on the side of the road in Homestead, Florida. They ran the plate and saw that the car was registered to me, but there was no sign of Genette. I had the car towed back to Fort Lauderdale and had to have the car fixed and the interior completely redone and then I managed to get rid of it and get out of the lease.

After that I never heard from her again, but did hear that several years later she married some other wealthy man living in Tennessee. Apparently, that was her MO—to find someone who could completely take care of her like all the other men in her life had done. She was totally incapable of doing anything except looking beautiful and performing sexually.

During the whole time I was seeing Genette, I never took her to my apartment. I only took her to the yacht where several times we spent the weekend, but I never wanted to take her to the apartment because I feared when she saw how nice it was she would want to move in and was I glad I didn't!

CHAPTER 22

It was now late July 2001. I was glad to have gotten rid of Genette because she was becoming a real burden and a financial drain. It was clear that the husbands she had gone through had spent a lot of money on maintaining her lifestyle and just taking care of her. No man, unless he was incredibly wealthy, could keep that up for long.

As July turned into August, I went on several more cruises up to Alaska. On these cruises I didn't need anyone and I only did my training. I remember staying in Ketchikan for a week where all I did was walk down to the ships every day as they came in up the inner passage, train the crew, and then do the same thing the next day.

One afternoon after the training, I decided to go for a hike in the mountains behind the hotel in Ketchikan. It was a nice afternoon and actually was kind of warm so I started hiking up the trail into the foothills leading up the mountain. It was beautiful and quiet. Suddenly I heard the crackling of branches not too far away from me and when I turned around I saw a black bear! It scared the hell out of me and I froze.

The bear was about two hundred yards from me, but I could see it had cubs and it was looking for food. I didn't know what to do, whether to stand there frozen in fear or to run for my life. For a few minutes I stood there quietly, hoping the bear wouldn't see me. Then it looked up and looked directly at me; it knew I was there.

It started coming in my direction and I was so scared I ran like the wind down the trail and never looked behind me. I know you're told never to run because the bear could outrun you, but believe me I was running so fast I can't imagine the bear could run as fast as I was. I never even looked behind me. I heard the branches rustling, but again I never looked behind me and ran as fast as I could down the trail, hyperventilating all the way.

I finally got to the bottom where the trailer park was. I look behind me at that point but did not see anything. Thank God. It must have turned around and gone away. I was shaking like a leaf when I got back to the hotel. That was the last hike I would ever take in that direction, let alone into the woods on my own. After everything I had been through, the last thing I needed was to be eaten by a bear!

The week went by and I made my way back to Fort Lauderdale to stay around the office for the last week of August and the first week of September. It was quiet and I did family things with my kids and Kristen when I wasn't running all over the world leading a double life. It took its toll more on me than it did on anyone else.

When I was home, I spent time in the office lining up cruises, and then I usually went home in the afternoon when Kristen got home and the kids got home from school. We would go eat pizza as a family and, in spite of all my running around, I seldom missed any holidays, birthdays, or anniversaries.

During the last week of August, my son Chet told me he wanted to go to a Catholic high school and I made it my goal to get him in there. He was raised Protestant so it was a little tricky, but I managed to speak to the chancellor of the high school. Chet had to write a letter that was convincing enough so that they would admit him so he could start in September with the rest of his friends.

That letter was the best thing I ever did for him. He excelled in the school and he and his friends all went on to the University of Florida at Gainesville. He graduated with honors and has a highly successful career. At least I did one thing right.

Labor Day of 2001 was quiet and we had a barbecue at Kristen's parents' house in Fort Lauderdale. They lived right off Oakland Park Boulevard in a small ranch house. During the time that I was gone, Kristen would spend time with her mother going to craft fairs and to the festival flea market off the Florida Turnpike in Delray Beach. It all seemed to work—at least I wanted to believe it did.

We were still living in the little condominium in Davie, Florida, and for the moment, everything seemed okay. Because I still had the yacht and the apartment, I always had a place to go if I needed to get away for a few days. My cruises were in such quick succession that no one knew where I was and exactly when I was coming back. Things always changed. Many times the cruise lines would fly me directly out to another vessel, sometimes one right after another.

The merry-go-round was beginning to take its toll on me and my family and things were getting progressively worse. Somehow, I managed to keep it all together, but then came the infamous day of September 11, 2001.

The morning started off normally. I went to the office around seven AM, put on coffee, turned on some music, and began to check emails and make some morning phone calls. Usually every morning that I was there I would walk across Andrews Avenue to the Reno Diner where I would get a fried egg sandwich and French fries. I will never forget walking across the street, waiting in line to order my sandwich, having it cooked fresh, and then going into the seating area while I watched the morning news.

I, along with everyone else, saw the bulletin saying the first plane had crashed into the Twin Towers. Everyone was glued to the TV. It was thought the first impact was an accident, but right before our eyes the second plane appeared and smashed into the second tower. At this point everyone suspected that it was a terrorist attack and, as we all know, that's exactly what was. Everyone was horrified. Everything came to a standstill. When I say everything, I mean everything. Within minutes we heard sirens out on the street.

Port Everglades was shut down, as was the Fort Lauderdale International Airport. The National Guard was in position at the port where all the oil tanks were stored, to make sure that no one would get in there to set off a bomb. Nobody knew exactly what was happening, but we all knew we were under attack.

All the cruise ships in port that day were put on lockdown and all the cruises were canceled. All the airlines were grounded, and we all know that within an hour, absolutely no planes were in the air other than military fighter jets guarding the capital while the President circled around in Air Force One.

This, for all of us, was worse than any nightmare that could be imagined. After the second tower was hit and went down, I went back across the street. Judy was crying in the office and her boyfriend Frank, a sergeant in the Fort Lauderdale Police Department, was there. He was on his way to the airport, where many officers had been summoned to create a perimeter while the National Guard did the rest. Army trucks and jeeps and light weapons were coming down federal highways and being put in position all over the port and near the airport.

Our phones went silent and we all left the office to go home. The nation was on high alert and all the kids got sent home from school with police escorts guarding the buses. Because Kristen worked for the police department, she was on emergency duty and ordered to stay through the night. They had provisions for this in the event of just such a national disaster.

I went home. Sergio and Chet were home and we all watched TV as this tragic story unfolded. We watched the firefighters running for their lives as the buildings collapsed and then we watched George Bush address the nation to say they knew who did this and they would hear us coming. It seemed like an eternity as the evening went on into the next day and then into the next day. Then the bulletin came on with the pictures of the air assault on Baghdad, the campaign of shock and awe. The goal was to take out the Iraqis and to kill Saddam Hussein. As we all know, he proved to be elusive but eventually was caught and executed. As history will catalog it, the Iraqis were not the culprits.

Everything was on lockdown for several weeks and many businesses even closed. The cruise lines suspended all of my training cruises until further notice and I actually had no idea when they would resume again. People were not flying and planned vacations were being canceled due to fear of the ship being blown up while going out of port or in the open ocean by an enemy submarine.

The cruise lines from Fort Lauderdale to Miami to Port Canaveral to the Port of Tampa were all shut down for a minimum of three weeks. This was financially devastating not only to them but to me as well. In three weeks my company went from making a hundred thousand dollars a month down to between $5000 and $8000 a month. This was unbelievable, and the fact that it happened in such a short time was even more unbelievable!

Throughout these weeks stories of heroism, rescues, and funerals filled the airwaves. There essentially was no regular programming.

I don't know how we got through it but we did. The airport eventually opened up and flights resumed, although many were on limited schedules and many were flying with very few passengers. The travel and vacation industry had been paralyzed. Fort Lauderdale, including Port Everglades was a ghost town and seemed as if it was under occupation.

The National Guard had set up checkpoints at all locations going in and out of the port and this alone deterred anyone from going there unless it was for fuel delivery or some other necessary service.

When the cruise lines began to sell again, it was on a very limited schedule and the ships were escorted out of Port Everglades by gunboats carrying machine guns, just in case there was an attack on the slow-moving vessels as they departed into the open ocean. Many of the ships sailed with less than half of the capacity that they could take. The cruise lines lost millions during that time.

It was now October and I had absolutely no schedule for training or for hazardous waste removal on any of the ships. As a matter fact, I was told that there would be no discussion about future training until the beginning of 2002. I was essentially out of business until then.

What could I do? I had been living on $40-50,000 a month to pay all the bills, maintain the yacht, the office, the apartment, and everything else that went along with it. All of a sudden, I did not have the money to pay for it. For the six previous years I had made over a million dollars a year and hadn't saved a penny of it because I thought it would never end. I guess I'm not the only one that ever made that mistake, but now that the party was over I sure wish I had been wiser.

I tried to get loans at several banks, but because I was essentially the company and there were no real assets, I was declined for everything. As November and December came, we were still receiving payments from work that had been done in the late summer prior to 9/11, but the money was drying up fast and I was unable to pay many of the bills.

I negotiated deferred payment plans with many of the people I owed money to and that seemed to work for a little while—it bought me a few months. But as I looked ahead to February and March of 2002, the end was near.

In late January, my copy machine salesman, a guy named Barry, came into the office to ask me about payment on the copy machines that

I owned or was leasing. He knew that the business had essentially dried up because of 9/11, but the finance companies wanted the payments on the machines that we had used to create the training manuals. We had three state-of-the-art Minolta color copiers that we used to make the books. The payments were all around $250 a month, but I didn't have the money.

For some reason Barry never looked rattled, even during this time when everyone in every business was doing poorly. Car sales had fallen off and all service businesses had slowed down because people in that area lost revenue because tourism had fallen off. Fort Lauderdale Beach was empty during the time when usually every restaurant and store was packed all along the beach. Again, everyone was just staying home and canceling their vacations.

Barry sat in my office and told me, after listening to me, how he thought he could help me.

I said, "How can you help me?"

He said, "Easy, I will use your credit to get copy machines for my customers who won't qualify, and I will pay you $10,000 for each lease that gets approved." My credit was still good enough because we had managed to squeak by making minimum payments during this entire time without my score going into the toilet.

Barry said he would be back to talk to my secretary about how to set this entire thing up. Two days later he came back with all the forms and told her just how to fill everything out whenever he brought in a customer so that they would qualify for the copy machine based on my credit. The machine would be delivered and then he would bring me a check or cash for $10,000.

This seemed like a miracle and too good to be true! Actually, it was true—it worked very well. Within the first week, he brought me four contracts and we sent in my Social Security number and they were all approved. His clients got the machines and I got the money. The machines were first delivered to my office and then Barry hired a truck and brought them to his clients' offices. What a perfect setup! All of a sudden, I began to accrue cash again.

The only downside to this was that in forty-five days I had to start making the minimum payments on all of the copy machines. Remember, they were all in my name with my Social Security number and credit backing the leases up.

Within forty-five days, Barry brought us twenty-six contracts that netted us $260,000 in cash to float the company, pay our bills, make the minimum payments on the copy machines, and to keep us going even though we had no training. Then in April 2002, the cruise lines began to do some limited training again. I was generating money; little as it might be, it was better than nothing.

The $260,000 went pretty fast. We took care of things as they came in, but several payments were very large, especially to the waste disposal companies that took away what we got off the cruise ships. These bills had to be paid because of the regulatory and compliance aspects that the cruise lines would be subject to. This was something that could not be fooled around with.

The payments to the waste disposal companies were over a hundred thousand dollars and I paid them all. Now we were only working with $160,000 and the limited amount of money generated from the cruise lines from the training classes they were allowing me to do.

It wasn't like the old days. The training was limited to one day in port and I only made maybe $2000 or $3000 tops, maybe $5000 in a week, and did not travel on the ships at all. They were doing their best to fill all the cabins and get everybody back into the cruising mood after the whole 9/11 nightmare.

It was now the summer of 2002, and we were making all twenty-six minimum payments on a monthly basis back to the finance companies that backed up the copy machines. As long as we made the payments, nobody bothered us and Barry continued to bring us contracts that I would front for the $10,000 that he would pay us. It actually worked and worked very well. We were now up to forty-five machines that required about $12,000 a month payout, but as long as he kept bringing us a contract or two for the minimum payments, we were ok.

This was some financial spiral. There was no way we could keep it up, but we did it as long as we could. The minimum payments were mounting up and because we had gone to every one of these finance companies several times they finally began to get wise and were declining the loans on the copy machines. This is what Barry feared might happen and he warned me about it.

At this point Barry said I should take whatever money I had left and buy art. He had many fine pieces of work hanging in his home that would be worth hundreds of thousands of dollars that he could take off the wall and sell at any time to a collector. This was his form of hidden wealth. He had been doing this for years so his art collection was worth several million dollars. Whenever he needed money, he would liquidate a famous painting or sell a piece of fine jewelry for cash.

He was a real operator, but Barry was from Brooklyn and was about the most street-smart guy I ever met. He had a mustache, a toupee, a fat stomach, elevator shoes, and a lot of jewelry and he always had his shirt open so you could see the gold chains around his neck. He was a real character to say the least.

The copy machine scam was over. We had reached its limit and could not get any more financing. Now we were stuck with $14,000 a month in minimum copy machine payments and only $120,000 left in the bank. With all the monthly bills to maintain the apartment, the yacht, and all the other stuff including the minimum payments, we were going down fast. As opposed to buying art, I had another idea. This one was a real lulu!

CHAPTER 23

Because we were running out of money, I knew I had to start some kind of business with some of the money that I had left. We were on a short fuse because, although we had $120,000 in the bank because of the copy machines, payments going out were in excess of $25,000 a month and the environmental training business was minimal to say the least.

As a matter fact, many of the cruise lines were hiring their own environmental officers on every ship, so they needed me less and less. I had actually trained all of these people at one time or another during the past seven years and now they were taking over my job.

If we were making $5000 a month from the cruise lines, we were making a lot. The business was dying right before my eyes. I was looking in the paper one day and saw an ad that said "adult toy business for sale." He had a phone number to call, so I called.

It turned out this guy up in North Fort Lauderdale had a warehouse with fifteen pallets of adult sex toys, including blowup dolls and artificial vaginas, all for sale including a website that they could all be sold on. He said that the business could be purchased for $15,000 and if all the toys were sold, whoever bought it would make over $180,000.

I took a ride up to meet him and look at all the inventory. Sure enough, he had a warehouse with all these boxes labeled, tagged, and inventoried with every conceivable sex toy you can imagine. Everything was priced, organized, catalogued, and in the computer so you knew exactly what each item cost and how to find it on the website. The price of the business included all of the software cataloging and inventory control. That way all the sales could be monitored.

It seemed like it would work. He didn't want the business anymore because he was sick. He had learned that he had leukemia and decided to sell.

He had purchased all the stuff from China and it had just been shipped there in a container. I was genuinely interested. I took my secretary to see the operation and look at the software. The only kick was that they hadn't sold one thing yet because the business had never really gotten started. All he wanted was $15,000, but to me that was a lot of money that I did not have to waste.

Judy and I went back and forth four times before I decided that we would do this. She said she could monitor the website and based on the way everything was tagged, we could find it and then ship it out. The customers would pay us with PayPal and everything seemed like it would work okay. With the possibility of turning $15,000 into $180,000, this seemed like potentially a pretty profitable little business that might save us.

I got a cashier's check for $15,000 and my son Sergio and his friends rented a box truck and went to the warehouse to move all of the pallets down to our warehouse in Fort Lauderdale. Now we were in the adult toy business!

Holy shit, from doing training on cruise ships to selling blowup dolls and fake pussies? I guess you could say we had diversified in our business model!

Judy got all the software and we began to set the whole thing up online. One problem was that the domain name was not easy to find, and in order to come up on the first page of search results, we would have had to pay a company several thousand dollars a month to maintain internet visibility on a daily and weekly basis. This became clear after only a few weeks of messing around with the software, the website, and the domain name. What a nightmare!

I found the guy we bought the company from and complained, but he said that was our problem because we never brought it up before we bought the products. He was right. I even got a lawyer to see if I could get him for somehow misrepresenting what I had bought, but that wasn't the case.

He had been honest with us. I just didn't know enough to ask the right questions, especially how someone would find our site so they could buy one of our products.

Judy did the best she could trying to rearrange things to make it so people could find our adult site easier, but it didn't work. In the space of four or five weeks, we only got six or seven sales that didn't amount to more than a couple of hundred dollars. This was devastating. We had a whole warehouse full of the stuff and now we couldn't sell it. The money was going out and it was clear we were going down the drain.

During this time my son and his friends and even Judy began to open some of the pallets and take some of the toys and either use them or give them to their girlfriends, and then they would put a show on in my office when I wasn't there in the evening. My son and his friends used the dildos on their girlfriends and Judy was going into the office at night and making her boyfriend use the toys on her! This was kinky, but this is what they were doing.

It was hot in the warehouse and some of the toys and the packaging were beginning to buckle, as were the pallets. The heat and humidity damaged many of the items and now they were becoming worthless. I asked Judy to figure out something fast so we could get rid of these things before they were all destroyed and had no value. By the grace of God, she ran an ad on Craigslist and found some guy who actually came in and bought all the remaining items that were not damaged for $11,000.

I couldn't believe it. I had gone on a limited training cruise and when I came back everything was gone. He had come with his own truck and had taken everything away. He even took the software to develop their exclusive new website. They had the money to support it and make it. I had to hand it to her. She salvaged what she could, but we were still on the fast track to going down the chute.

We were now approaching the end of 2002 and, quite frankly, I wasn't interested in getting involved with any women. My priority was trying to salvage the company or at least salvage myself from total financial ruin.

By the end of 2002, I got another idea to use the yacht to do burials at sea. This meant taking out an urn with the ashes of a deceased person and having a funeral on the boat as the family watched the ashes going into the water and dispersing.

I created a brochure and visited all of the funeral homes in the Fort Lauderdale area with my captain's uniform on. Believe it or not, this was met with some reasonable success. I charged $750 for each burial at sea, which took about four hours. The family would come down to where the boat was docked, board the vessel, take the ashes out into the ocean, and have a ceremony with music. It was nice and everyone liked it.

People flew in from all over the country to have the ceremony performed. I got many references from funeral homes and left my brochures and business cards with them for families that wanted to take advantage of this service.

From the end of 2002 until mid-2003, I began to do burials at sea, sometimes five or six a month, netting me close to $5000. This wasn't bad, considering I had no real business at the company. Judy and Sergio kept the company open, while I did the burials at sea with a girl named

Carla I had hired as first mate. There was nothing romantic with us. She was just my helper on the cruises and she took care of the people as they came aboard and made sure everyone was safe while we conducted the ceremony. It worked out well.

During the holiday season of 2002 and 2003, I was inundated with requests for burials at sea. I performed over fifteen short cruises during a two-month period. This was great! I was making a living at this and it wasn't hard. But I could barely pay for the boat because the payment was $2200 a month and I still had to pay for the small condominium we lived in, in addition to the rent on the office and our cars. Kristen worked at the police department, so she made $1800 a month, and that money all went into the pot to keep us alive. At this point I gave up the apartment on the Intracoastal and the reality that the end of the line was near finally settled in.

While I had a good reputation with all the funeral homes, the burials at sea were getting sporadic. Sometimes I would get two or three in a row and all of a sudden for a week it would go dry, but I would always get called. Even four years later, I was still getting phone calls about whether or not I did burials at sea.

I was a safe captain and never compromised going out in dangerous weather or unpredictable seas. People seemed to appreciate that.

In late January 2003, I had to get an additional job in order to make money. I had met the general manager of World Ford, a large Ford dealership in Pembroke Pines, Florida. He told me to go down there and he would hire me as a salesman. He said all of his guys were making between $7000 and $8000 a month.

This seemed too good to be true, but I went down there and signed up. They put me through an automotive sales training school and I must say, it taught me how to buy a car and how to sell a car. I use what I learned to this day when negotiating any kind of car deal. There is no such thing as a good deal. The dealer always wins.

This dealership was gigantic. They sold almost five hundred cars a month and the pressure on every salesman was unbelievable. There were 67 salesmen at this dealership and the place was open seven days a week from seven in the morning until the last car pulled out of there at night. That could be one or two in the morning depending upon the last deal. Several times I didn't leave until one in the morning, after screwing on somebody's license plates as they left the dealership.

I was working at the dealership all week long. When I had a day off, I would do a burial at sea if I could, and the rest of the time I was at the Ford dealership trying to sell cars. In spite of the fact that there were so many salesmen, I did pretty well. I was averaging four to five cars a week and receiving checks directly from Ford Motor Company. On a weekly basis, I was making $1200-$1300, plus the checks in the mail that I got from Ford.

I learned how to get people to buy from me based on my knowledge of automobiles and my personality. It all seemed to work.

During this time, I was focused on just working and trying to survive, but there was a very attractive lady that worked in the business office. She was the right-hand person to the general manager of the dealership. Whenever we had a meeting, she would stand up and talk about the dealership's numbers and how good we were doing, but how much better we had to do.

I had the eye for her and she had the eye for me I could tell. She was married but apparently had had several affairs with some of the guys in the dealerships and they all said she was a hot ticket. She had all the trimmings of all the women I had been with, but I didn't want to get tangled up in something that I couldn't afford, especially considering that financially I was on thin ice.

One day, I decided against my better judgment to ask her to lunch. She accepted and she knew exactly why I wanted to take her in the car. She got in the car and I could immediately smell her perfume as I looked her over.

Boy, she looked good. She had a cute little body and was put together very well. She had beautiful teeth, a great smile, beautiful hands, nice features, and she knew just how desirable she was. I could tell she was no amateur.

Her name was Diane and we had lunch as I beat around the bush talking about just how attractive she was and how attracted I was to her. She also admitted that she had been giving me the eye the whole time I was at the dealership. I must say, though, at the end of our lunch before we got back to the dealership, we made out in the car for a little bit, with her giving me a very deep tongue kiss.

Once the kiss was through, she said to me that she knew it wasn't a good idea for us to start an affair because it would be something that we couldn't finish and she had no desire to get caught up in a losing proposition. Wow! She was the first woman who ever told me anything like that. I had to give her credit because she was smart enough to recognize it and move away.

After lunch we remained friendly, but only at a distance and that was that. I stayed at the dealership for several months when I got the idea that I could make more money at a more upscale dealership. I went over to Bayview Cadillac on Federal Highway and applied for a sales position there. I got all dressed up in a suit, went to the general manager, and asked him if he had any openings. He said they made openings for the right people but, at this dealership, there were only twelve salespeople who had been there for over thirty years. They all had a following and I would have to develop my own customers and not take anyone that they had sold a car to in the past.

I accepted the position even though I knew I didn't have the following, and I would rely on walk-ins as the more senior sales guys would allow me to have them. I left Ford and said goodbye to the 67 salesmen and working 80 hours a week.

At this point it was early July 2003 and hotter than hell down in southern Florida. I went to Cadillac. They gave me a nice office and they were also closed on Sundays. This was great! It was a close-knit group and the guys for the most part were pretty nice. They gave me some walk-ins and allowed me to stand on the service drive to try to convince customers to trade their cars if they needed too much service work or if they were older. The clientele at this dealership were mostly elderly people who had a lot of money and traded in their cars every two years whether they needed to or not.

Car prices were high and the commission was good, so it wasn't hard to make a couple of thousand dollars on the sale of the car plus the extras, which would include commission for financing and any options that they would buy. Many of the customers would buy vogue tires and wheels as well as fancy grills. This sometimes made my commission $3500 on a new car.

I wasn't doing that bad. I was averaging four to five thousand a month and I was actually making a living. I still had the yacht and I was still doing the burials at sea when I could. I was averaging one or two burials every two weeks so it was better than nothing.

Sergio and Judy had to close the company down in late May 2003 and I wasn't there to witness any of it. They sold all the furniture and everything else we had as we had no additional business from the cruise lines and were unable to pay the rent and any of the other bills. It was very sad.

Sergio and Judy stayed right till the last day, when the landlord took the keys and whatever was left was turned over to him. Luckily, I was able to get them both a position with a small company in Davie that did similar work to what we did, so at least they had jobs.

While I was at Cadillac, I still would go to some nautical meetings that various groups had around town. One afternoon when I got off at the dealership at three, I went down Dania Beach to a little bar where they were having a meeting and I met Joanie.

She was a little operator in the community, who was pretty good-looking and had lived in town for over twenty years. She worked at the Captain's Nautical Training Center on Federal Highway in Dania Beach. This was a landmark facility that had simulators to teach captains and pilots how to dock cruise vessels and cargo ships. It was a world-renowned facility and Joanie had a long-time affair going with the Director of the Operations. His name was Stan.

Joanie was a real piece of work. She knew she was attractive and she used every bit of that attraction to hook up with anyone that would spend money on her, buy her a good dinner, or take her to get her nails done. She wasn't that easy to go to bed with because she was sleeping with Stan on a regular basis and she was his main squeeze.

It was well known around Dania Beach and at the school that they were an item. She pretended that she wasn't with him, but she was.

She and I hit it off right away as we had a lot to talk about. She was very much into social climbing as well as just liked to be with new men. She was pretty, bubbly, and very well put together. She was sexy in her own way and had a very attractive personality. She was smart and savvy and knew just how to turn it on and turn it off. She was a real businesswoman who had started up several small companies and medical clinics on her own. She had been in the medical industry for over twenty years and was a registered nurse.

I told her that I had a yacht, was a yacht captain, and that I had done all of the environmental training for all the cruise lines and had sailed all over the world for nine years. I also told her I was now selling cars at Cadillac. She wasn't quite sure what to believe because she didn't understand how could I possibly own a yacht and work selling cars. I told her I did own a yacht and that I would bring it down to the marina so she could see it.

She said, "Okay, let's go out on a Saturday so I can see this yacht. In fact, I would like to bring my whole family out for a ride so you can meet my mother, brothers, and my daughter."

I said okay.

Saturday came and I told Kristen that I had to take care of some business and go on a cruise for a burial. I took the boat down to the marina at 17th Street where I met Joanie and her family as they boarded my yacht. When I pulled in, she was visibly impressed as I was wearing my captain's uniform with my four bars. I docked the boat perfectly and then tied it up on my own.

She greeted me with a big smile and hug, and then introduced me to everyone in her family. They were all impressed by the yacht and all of its amenities. I had three color televisions on it, two full showers, two full bedrooms and bathrooms, a large upper helm, and open-air deck. It was a great boat for being outside on a beautiful day. That's exactly why I was hanging onto the yacht in spite of my financial difficulties. It was pretty hard to give this thing up, considering I had had it now for over four years.

Everyone boarded the yacht and we shoved off. We went under the 17th Street Bridge, out into the port, then out into the ocean. It was a little choppy, so we made a turn and came back into the port and continued down through the Intracoastal Pass where all the cruise ships were docked on that Saturday afternoon.

We passed all the ships including the Royal Caribbean, Holland America, and Carnival vessels—all parked, getting ready to leave at five o'clock that afternoon. We sailed down the Intracoastal very slowly, all the way to Dania Beach, where we stopped and docked at a pizza place. When her brother was getting off the boat, his glasses fell off and went to the bottom. He dove in the water and retrieved them without a problem. He came up soaking wet. We got him a towel as we went in to order pizza. It was a totally beautiful afternoon as we all sat outside eating our pizza and watching the seagulls fly by. I got along well with her family and she became a friend for life. I'm still friends with her to this day and she still has two or three men she is juggling at sixty-three!

CHAPTER 24

Joanie was very interesting. While she had a long-term ongoing affair with Stan at the nautical school, she always seemed to have a parade of men fighting for her attention. She was a little social butterfly in the town of Dania Beach and went to lots of networking events. In addition, she was involved in the medical community, so she met lots of doctors that were involved in alternative medicine or something else that she could sink her teeth into. She was always trying to make money and get taken out to dinner at the same time.

The only reason she was hanging around Stan was to ensure long-term job security, filing all of the insurance claims from the nautical school. Stan was much older than she was and had been divorced for a long time. He was very troubled and Joanie seemed to be his consolation. On a regular basis, she would go down to his house near the beach and sleep with him as the situation called for it. When things got a little tense with the Board of Directors at the school, and it seemed as if they were trying to eliminate her position, she would sleep with Stan and make sure he went to bat for her to protect her job. It always seemed to work.

I began to see Joanie on and off after we went out on the boat. She loved the ocean so she definitely wanted to stay in good graces with me. I was a little bit different than Stan and I think she found me refreshing compared with the other men going in and out of her life.

She would invite me to her house for dinner when it was convenient and if she didn't have other plans. She was very careful to make sure Stan was out of town, or at a board meeting that would go till very late in the evening. She knew just how to play her cards right.

Initially we would have cordial dinners which would include her, her daughter, her mother, and sometimes her brothers. It was all very friendly and above board. She was just being my friend, although I could tell that from time to time, little hints of romance would come up.

Sometimes she called me up and asked me if I would take her out on the boat. Because I was working at the car dealership, my time was very limited and usually I was only available one day during the week and on a Sunday. I was still married to Kristen and during this time I stayed closer to home than I used to. The company had closed and my funds were limited. By this point, I only had about $25,000 left to my name.

Joanie could not understand how I could own yacht and only work at a car dealership. I explained to her that I had owned a company where I sailed all over the world and did environmental training for the cruise lines, but with 9/11 and everything else, the company had gone under. I was still able to keep the boat—at least for now.

It was now late summer and Joanie loved to lie out on the deck of my yacht and take her top off. She was a little tease in this regard. When we were out on the boat, she wanted me to take her to Shooters or up to Houston's on the Intracoastal for lunch or an early dinner. She knew how to spend money and figured that she would spend whatever money I had left, if I let her.

I was still doing funerals at sea, though they were few and far between, and sometimes she came along with me. Her only goal was to enjoy being out on the ocean and getting some sun.

Our relationship was very platonic until one night when I took her over to the Diplomat Hotel on Hollywood Beach for dinner. They seated us at a romantic table overlooking the ocean. We had a couple of drinks and a beautiful dinner. She was a little loaded when I brought her home and she invited me into her house and then into her bedroom. She said she just wanted to lie down with me for a little while and that was it.

Well, you know that was a lie. Suddenly she started kissing me and then asked me to kiss her "girls." She referred to her female parts in the third person. Her breasts were her girls and her vagina was "she." Joanie directed me to kiss both of her girls and her girls' nipples. Then she told me that "she," her pussy, wanted me to kiss her, too.

At first I didn't know what the hell she meant. Then she told me she wanted me to go down on her, especially after hearing all of my wild stories on the cruise lines. With that I licked her pussy like it had never been licked before! She went crazy! She said that nobody had ever done that to her like that and she was shocked at just how good I was. She came multiple times and was out of control.

Now I had myself another situation to deal with and Joanie wasn't easy at all. She was a real handful with all of her boyfriends, her relationship with Stan, and the fact that she was so elusive and noncommittal. I never knew when she was available or what kind of a mood she'd be in when I finally hooked up with her.

It turned out that I would see her once or twice a week. Usually on my day off, I would see her in the early afternoon and would eventually wind up back at her house where she would ask me to go down on her again. Apparently, I had some real value there that she didn't want to lose. I also wound up spending money I didn't have, taking her to different places for lunch or dinner.

As the summer progressed, we got a little closer and we would go down to Las Olas Boulevard at various times and meet for breakfast or brunch. She was chatty, vivacious, and always into some kind of a business deal that never materialized into anything. I found myself falling for her because in a certain way she was like a mirror image of me. She knew how to maneuver her way around with a lot of men in her sphere of influence. With all of the men she had around her, I never crossed paths with any of them. She knew how to time everything just right.

In early September, I had to take a trip to North Carolina because I was trying to get a new job and a friend of mine that owned the company asked me to come up there to talk to him about it. It was about a ten-hour drive and I asked Joanie if she wanted to go with me. She jumped at the chance and said, "Yes, I'd love to!" She was never one to pass up a good time.

We planned the trip to take four days. We would stay in St. Augustine the first night and then make our way up to Charlotte where we would stay for two nights and then back down to Fort Lauderdale on the fourth day. This was our first time staying in a hotel for an extended period of time. When we left, we got two large ice cream cones and hit the road. We were playing music and singing in the car as we drove up Interstate 95 toward St. Augustine, Florida. We were holding hands and stealing kisses all along the way.

We got to the hotel, checked in, and immediately started making love. She was very sensual and I think she considered me a new find amongst her collection of men that had fallen for her. I could tell she was smitten by me as well. By the time we went to dinner, it was about seven o'clock in the evening. We ate at a little restaurant along the water and then walked along the Fort as the sun set. We were having a good time with each other and it seemed like she was really into me. But this was her style; she knew exactly how to make whoever she was with feel like the most important person in the world at that moment.

The next morning, we drove to Charlotte and went to my friend's company. He received both of us very well and, after he and I met, he led us back to his lake house. We met his wife and all went out to dinner.

The next day we all went jet-skiing on the lake. We shared the watercraft and Joanie sat behind me and held onto me very tightly as we drove up and down the lake. I must say, I was feeling closer and closer to her.

After we finished playing on the lake, we went back up to the house and had a barbecue and drinks. Everyone started getting a little drunk and my friend made a move on Joanie. He told her she was very hot and he wanted to do her. She got insulted, slapped him, and then asked me to take her back to the hotel—which I did.

My friend was shocked because, apparently, he had never been rejected before. His wife knew that this is what he would do because she was hoping that if they got it on so would we, meaning me and her. Wow! I never expected this, but he being rejected took care of any job possibilities I would have with him. In the morning when I called him, he told me that he was highly insulted by Joanie and that I should never bring her back again.

The next morning, we headed back to Florida. We had a good time going back, but we both were still in shock that they actually wanted to swap partners without thinking about it twice. As we drove along, we stopped at various sites along the way and then stopped in Jacksonville for the evening. We hugged and kissed and made passionate love as she referred to all of her female parts in the third person and how she wanted me to satisfy her in every way possible. During the ride back she told me she was falling in love with me and I actually began to believe her.

I had promised myself I wasn't going to get involved with anybody like this ever again, but as usual, I didn't take my own advice.

When we got home I dropped her off, but I was feeling jealous because I knew that as soon as she got to work the next morning she would see Stan and they would start their whole thing again. Not only was she seeing Stan, she was also seeing some doctor that she was trying to get involved with so he would open a clinic that she could be in charge of.

Joanie knew how to work everything to her benefit. The fact that she was a little manipulator enticed me to keep going after her. It was a vicious cycle and, of course, this lit my candle along with the allure of the sex and romantic encounters.

I was still working at the car dealership, but as soon as I got off work I found myself driving down to Joanie's house, circling around the block, seeing if she was home, then going down to the sea school to see if I could locate her car. Many times, she was nowhere to be found until I finally went past Stan's house down by the water. Her Ford Explorer would be parked behind his house where she thought that I couldn't see it because she knew I was hot on her trail.

I would call her cell phone but she wouldn't answer and then later that evening at about eleven o'clock she would text me back to tell me she was unavailable. No kidding? This whole routine started to drive me crazy; then of course, I was leaving my own house with Kristen wondering where I was going now that I didn't have to go on any cruises. I always made up some story about going on an interview or trying to get a new job. I must admit the excuses were getting pretty lame, but she still never said a word.

The money was running out and I was unable to pay for the yacht anymore. I didn't tell anyone, but I began to default on the payments. The finance company threatened to repossess the boat if more than five payments were missed. When the fifth payment came due, I couldn't pay it and one morning, a captain and the sheriff showed up at my door, asked for the keys to the boat, went down to where it was docked, and repossessed it. That was that, my beautiful yacht was gone after four years. I was heartbroken because that yacht had been my last bastion of living the life of luxury.

When I told Joanie the yacht was gone, she got upset and said that she would have to find a new boyfriend who had a yacht. Can you imagine? But then she started laughing and said, "But that's okay, John. You're still pretty cute, so I think I'll keep you around for a while, so you can take care of my girls when I want you to." What kind of a thing is that to say? That was terrible, but at least she was honest…

We continued to see each other on and off over the next few months. I was still working for the Cadillac dealership. Kristen and I were lucky enough to be able to pay the rent, two car payments, and the other bills including the credit cards that I had racked up during the time that the company was in business. I was trying to maintain our credit, but with the repossession of the yacht, I knew our credit was going to go down the toilet.

After assessing everything, I decided that it would be best to do a personal bankruptcy. I still had over 1.5 million dollars' worth of debt, including all the copy machines that I had defaulted on. That, combined with the deficiency from when they sold the yacht, told me it was time to file.

I went to a lawyer in downtown Fort Lauderdale and began the process. My schedule F, the form that you list all of your debts on, was 48 pages long. It was the largest bankruptcy that this particular lawyer had ever handled. Around this time, I was also getting collection notices as well as judgment notices served at my house. At times these were intimidating because they would threaten me with jail or immediate attachment of my personal bank account and whatever little money we had in it to pay our bills so we could survive.

If this wasn't bad enough, my son Sergio, who had worked with me in the company for nine years, went off the deep end. He was unable to cope with the fact that I wasn't rolling in dough anymore and that he couldn't do whatever he wanted. He began to drink and do drugs and got himself into a world of trouble. He was doing and selling Oxycontin and was getting out of hand. He began stealing jewelry from his mother and from anyone else that he could get anything from. He got fired from his job for being stoned and was literally unable to function unless he was high or drunk.

Judy, my old secretary, was working at the other company where I had gotten her and Sergio a job after my company folded. She was doing okay until she went to the doctor with a minor skin issue that turned out to be cancer. She had the spot removed, then another spot popped up in another place on her body. She had that one removed, but it turned out that the cancer had gotten into her lymph nodes. Now she was doomed.

She kept getting small operations that removed different sections of her lymph nodes and the cuts on her kept getting larger and deeper. She was actually told she probably only had eight to ten years to live unless she got chemotherapy and a more aggressive treatment, but she did not take the doctor's advice. She continued to smoke, drink, and do whatever she wanted.

She tried to help Sergio with his addiction, but she was dealing with her own problems and as her cancer rapidly progressed, she began to go downhill quickly. She continued to work, but took many days off because she was so tired she could barely get out of bed. In addition, she had two teenage daughters that depended on her for everything. Luckily her new employer was able to get a reasonable life insurance policy on her that he and his wife were kind enough to pay for. They both knew she wasn't going to last that long and the girls needed to be taken care of when she was gone. During that time, I would visit Judy and would take her to lunch if she was able to eat. We reminisced and laughed about all the insane things she helped with over the years, but both knew she was on a short fuse. Every time I dropped her off, I gave her a warm hug because I never knew if that was the last time I would ever see her again. In 2010, Judy lost her long battle with cancer. She was the best friend and confidant that anyone could have ever had. I shall never forget her and always miss her.

Joanie never knew I was married—she thought that I was divorced. Because I only saw her maybe once or twice a week, she never questioned what I was doing, simply because she didn't want to be questioned as to what she was doing. This seemed to work pretty well and I was the one who was getting carried away with trying to chase her all over town. Our lovemaking became very intense, but I think it was that way with whoever she was with. We continued to meet sometimes for breakfast and would go down to the water to talk by the beach on occasion, but things were beginning to change.

She kept complaining about Stan and made it known to me that the nature of their relationship was only so she could keep her job. She made no bones about it and actually I understood, although I was jealous and always knew when she was hanging out with him. I didn't have the money to take her out like I used to, so most of our meetings involved a quick drink, an ice cream cone, or something very simple and inexpensive.

This was not Joanie's normal relationship. She was always wined and dined and taken to the best places. Unless you did that, you weren't getting in her pants. With her there was always a price and she made that crystal clear.

On occasion, I would go to her house on Saturday when I was off. She would be making dinner for her mother and the rest of her family and I would just show up. They all seemed to like me and were even sympathetic to the fact that I didn't have the boat anymore and that I was going through some pretty tough times.

The bankruptcy filing was underway and I got a notice in the mail to appear at the bankruptcy court on a certain date. I was nervous, to say the least. Luckily, in the letter it said notices had been sent to all the collection agents. They stopped coming to my house. At least I didn't have to worry about that anymore.

CHAPTER 25

The date of the bankruptcy hearing was quickly approaching. I asked the lawyer what I should bring with me and he said, "Nothing, just bring you."

He said that the judge would ask me what happened. I should just tell him or her that my company had gone out of business and 9/11 was a real turning point when everything went down. I had hung onto the boat for as long as I could and when it was repossessed, I was down to only $4000 to my name.

In the bankruptcy filing, all of the credit cards as well as copy machines were listed, in addition to the mortgage on the Weston house which was now empty and had gone into foreclosure. Our automobiles and anything else that we had, except for some furniture and family heirlooms, were listed, but they were mostly Kristen's and not mine and had very little value if they had to be liquidated. The trustee didn't care about that stuff.

The date of the hearing arrived and my lawyer arrived with me at the courthouse. We waited in the room with many others that were in the same situation and waited for my name to be called. I went alone because Kristen had to go to work and I took time off from the car dealership.

The lawyer said that many of the creditors might be there, but he also said nobody might be there. That would be known when the judge would ask the audience in the hearing room if anyone was there based on my case.

It was a female judge and when she called my name, I stood up and went up in front of her with my attorney. She verified what was said and asked if anyone in the audience wanted to object to me filing a Chapter 7. Much to my amazement no one was there, no one from the credit card companies or the copy machine companies. That only took a minute and she looked at me, looked at my file, and then asked me what happened.

I told her I had had a thriving company until 9/11 hit and after that time we tried to survive in any way that we could. I did burials at sea using a yacht that I owned. It had been repossessed and after that we were barely surviving.

She said, "Discharged," and then said, "Next case!"

My lawyer and I walked out of the court and into the hall, and, boy, was I relieved. It was over! The bankruptcy gave me a fresh start, but now my credit was ruined and I had to rebuild it. This, of course, would take years.

I went home and decided that I would toe the line, try and stay close to my family, and do the right thing. I was seeing Joanie on and off, but the romantic relationship had turned into more of a friendship. When we did hang around together, it was usually in a business environment and nothing more. I found her interesting and she found me interesting, in spite of the fact that now I had nothing left except my ability to sell a couple of cars a week, which kept me going.

Throughout this time, I was worrying about my son. He had gotten several tickets for driving drunk and I was forced to get him out of jail several times during the previous three months.

He was living with his friends down the block from where we were, in a horrible two-room apartment that was really a drug den. They were doing drugs and dealing drugs and he was in a real spiral.

When his court dates came up, I had no money for an attorney and he had to get a public defender to represent him. Obviously, he didn't do very well. He had his license revoked, but he continued to drive without any regard for whether or not he had a license. He put his mother and me through hell, and this was only the beginning.

One night I went over to his apartment because I knew if I didn't do some kind of an intervention he would probably die or be killed in an accident. I took a baseball bat with me, knocked on the door, and when they didn't answer, I broke the door down, much to the surprise of the five or six stoned kids there. I began screaming like a maniac and breaking everything, telling them I was going to get the cops and have them all arrested if they didn't stop and that I was going to save my son, no matter what any of them would do.

They all thought I was nuts and began to make fun of me. I began really swinging my bat and whacked a couple of them in the head, including the main drug dealer, who happened to be there at that moment. He said he was going to get even with me as he ran out of the house. I began breaking windows and went wild so I would scare him into thinking that I was crazy, so he wouldn't bother my son anymore. That was a mistake.

The next evening, I was lying on the couch in my living room at about nine o'clock when a car came down my block and shots were fired right through my living room window, barely missing my head. For sure it was the drug dealers and his friends because my son verified that now he was out to get me.

After this incident I went to the police and worked closely with the narcotics agents to do a sting with the drug dealers who were selling the Oxycontin. My son was picked up by the officers and told that if he did not cooperate with them, he would go to jail for dealing drugs. If he cooperated, he would be released into my custody as long as I had him go to rehab in order to try and break his habit.

My son reluctantly agreed to be wired and sent into the house to make a drug buy that the agents could record in the car that was hiding around the block. I was in the squad car as well that night when they wired him, gave him $100, and told him to go in and make a buy. He was told to speak clearly and slowly so that the agents could hear everything via the wire. He went and did it. When he came out with the drugs, as soon as they verified that the hundred dollars was gone and he had the drugs in his possession, they took the drugs and immediately stormed the house.

They made several arrests including the main drug dealer who was from Tampa. I later learned that he got five years in the slammer because I never heard from him or any of them again.

Now my son had a chance to clean up his act, but he didn't. He still had a big supply of Oxycontin that he could use and his habit was somewhere around $100 to $150 a day. He had sporadic jobs but could only hold them for a week or two because of his behavior and not showing up because of his habit. As I mentioned, he would steal anything he could get his hands on in order to get money.

One day his best friend Frank called me up crying, saying that his grandfather's ring was missing and he was positive that Sergio had stolen it. His grandfather had given him the ring right before he died and this was very, very important to him. As soon as I got hold of Sergio, I asked him if he had taken the ring. He said no, of course, but he had and had hocked it at a local pawnshop and gotten $200 for it.

About the same time, Kristen had a ring go missing that had been passed down from her mother to her. It was valued at over $6000 and Sergio had hocked that ring as well. This time he got $1500. In his mind he was rich!

Kristen was a wreck after the ring went missing. Frank called the police and filed charges against Sergio for stealing his grandfather's ring. The cops got the ring back from the hock shop and returned it to Frank, then arrested Sergio for theft. I found out where Sergio had hocked his mother's ring, but this time it was too late because Sergio had not paid the maintenance fee for them to hold the ring. They had sold it and it was gone. There was nothing anyone could do.

Sergio was arrested for petty theft because the value was under a thousand dollars. Either way, he still had to appear in court and get a public defender. This kid was causing all kinds of problems wherever he went.

About this time, Judy, my old secretary and Sergio's friend, was dating a guy who was a project superintendent at a construction site on Fort Lauderdale Beach. I don't know how, but Sergio met him through Judy and he hired Sergio to be a watchman on the property. What a mistake!

Sergio could barely function during the day. He had nowhere to go so he lived at this guy's house and dragged himself up in the morning to go to work with him at the site. He was making pretty good money, but this was bad because this continued to feed his habit. He was now out of my control and did whatever he wanted and again he was going down fast.

This kid was twenty-two and could not get over the fact that I did not own a company anymore and the money did not flow freely like it used to. He and Judy's boyfriend got along well until it became clear that Sergio was undependable and couldn't be counted on to show up for work on time or to follow the rules—something he did not understand. He had taken total advantage of me when he worked for me and did pretty much whatever he wanted.

Once, when I still had the company, he and his friends didn't show up at the port when they were supposed to and didn't make a scheduled pickup for Norwegian Cruise lines. It caused me to lose a $400,000 account. This was only some of what went on. The stress of never knowing when and if they would show up would give anyone a heart attack. They were always either drunk, stoned, or with some girls. I fired them many times but I just kept taking them back like lots of fathers do when their son works for them. It's a vicious cycle. Never hire your kid and his friends!

Sergio lost his job with the construction company and was only picking up odd jobs here and there. He had to move back in with his mother and me because he had no money and nowhere else to go. He was still bumming drugs from his friends and when he couldn't get any more he would go out and somehow steal something that would enable him to get a fix. His habit was pretty bad and it showed no signs of slowing down.

I was still seeing Joanie on and off, but my main focus was trying to rescue Sergio and save his life. No matter how many times I tried to straighten him out, he would just fall back. I took him to counselors and I even got him into a community rehabilitation center. But nothing seemed to work. Finally, one of the counselors got him into a methadone program so he could wean away from the Oxycontin.

He didn't have a license so I had to drive him all the way up to Pompano Beach to the methadone clinic where it cost $11 a day for him to get his fix. This was seven days a week, $77 a week, money that I didn't have. Kristen was working at the police department and I was still working at the automobile dealership. I was selling cars, but not as many as I did in the past. I was only averaging three sales or about $2500 a month and that barely covered our rent, car payments, and living expenses. It was amazing going from making over $1 million a year down to about $500-600 a week!

We were renting our condominium for $1400 a month. This was cheap for South Florida at the time and believe me, this place was nothing special. It had three small bedrooms, a carport and was very dark inside. It had lots of termites and was about thirty years old. What Kristen made at the police department covered the rent, and what I made covered our other expenses. In the bankruptcy, they allowed us to keep the two cars as long as we made the payments. Other than that, we had no more debts, but we also had no more credit.

As part of my job, I was networking on behalf of the dealership. I would go to events around town and the dealership allowed me to join the Fort Lauderdale Chamber of Commerce. The company had long since folded and now all I had were stories about the cruise ships and all the places I had been. For the most part, when I started to speak about them, nobody believed that I had been to all those places around the world.

One hot and sticky Thursday morning, I was walking from the parking structure back to the showroom where they kept the new Cadillacs when I received a phone call from England. All I remember is that the phone rang but I did not see a number, only what looked like a European code of some sort. I said, "Hello."

The voice on the other end said, "This is Jonathan Peck, the owner of Killgerm Group in Dobcross, England. Are you the person who invented the light bulb crushing machine?"

When I said yes, he said that someone from the Holland America line had given him my phone number and he had been trying to get in touch with me for several months, but apparently he had been dialing the wrong digit. Now he said, "I finally found you and would like you to come to England so we can talk about assigning your patent on the invention to us at Killgerm Group."

I almost had a stroke! I could not believe what I was hearing! I said, "Please repeat that?"

He said again, "We would like to have you assign your invention to us and have you work for us as a consultant. During that time, we will build the product and launch it into the marketplace. You will be in charge of the whole program. I will make arrangements for you to come to England so we can put this deal together. Is this something you would agree to?"

I said yes, of course, and asked when I would hear from him again. He asked me for my home address, reaffirmed my phone number, and said he would be back in touch with me soon.

I walked into the dealership in total disbelief at the call I had just received. I told one of the salesmen I was friends with, an older guy named Frank. He was happy for me and told me to go forward and take the deal.

At this point I didn't know what to do. I called Kristen and told her—she didn't believe me. Then, I called Joanie and told her I would meet her after I got out of the dealership for a drink. We met at Mangoes in Fort Lauderdale and I told her the whole story.

All of a sudden, she was interested in me like never before! She said, said, "Oh, John, you will become rich again! No one ever gets a phone call like that. It's amazing!"

I said I was still not sure what to believe. We had a drink and suddenly she kissed me passionately when I said I was going home. Oh boy, now she had her claws in me again. Maybe this time, she could cash in with "Little Johnny."

When I went home it was early and Kristen wanted to know exactly what was said. I told her the whole thing and she said, "Okay, let's see what happens."

I didn't know what to do, so I continued to go to the Cadillac dealership to sell cars, but every day I thought that I would be contacted by Jonathan from England, with instructions on what to do. I received my first phone call in early September and didn't hear back from him until mid-October. It felt like an eternity. Finally, in the mail I got a plane ticket to Manchester, England, with instructions as to who would pick me up, where I would be staying, for how long, and what we would discuss.

This was what I had been waiting for, another shot at the Golden Goose!

The next day I took the letter and showed Joanie. She was ecstatic because now she knew that this was for real. For the month and a half I had waited to hear from Jonathan, hope had begun to fade that this might not happen. The letter and the plane ticket showed and now I knew that it wasn't.

I was to leave on October 24 and come back to Fort Lauderdale the day after Halloween. I was also told to get in touch with the president of Killgerm's United States division, a man named James Schaefer, who ran the Killgerm affiliate in Sarasota called Pest West Inc.

Killgerm actually made pest control units, the kind you see in restaurants that catch and kill flies, which was their main business. Jonathan was interested in the bulb machine because he wanted to get into the environmental business and the bulb machine offered him that opportunity. I did some research on the company and found out that Jonathan was very wealthy, worth hundreds of millions of dollars.

As October 24 approached, I didn't quite know what to do about working at the car dealership. Frankly, I was sick of it and I was very excited about what redeveloping this product could do for me. I made contact with James Schaefer and drove over to Sarasota to meet him.

He was a nice guy and was very supportive of Jonathan getting involved with the bulb machine, and believed we could market it as a state-of-the-art environmental product to help solve the problem of crushing fluorescent light bulbs, while safely extracting the mercury.

I had patented the product several years earlier, but had never done anything with it. I was the sole patent holder and after doing some due diligence, Jonathan figured out that this would be a good, profitable venture.

James and I hit it off well and the following week, I was set to go to Dobcross, England, to meet Jonathan, his staff, and to solidify my deal.

The Monday before I left, I went to the dealership, spoke to the general manager, and told him I was leaving because of the invention and the fact that I had been summoned to England by a company that wanted to purchase it from me. He was very nice and wished me the best of luck.

I did not have a job and at this point had no promise from Jonathan other than that I was going to England to talk about a possible arrangement.

After hearing this, Joanie called me every day to find out what was going on and when I was leaving. I told her when I was leaving and where I was staying. She said okay, but didn't say much of anything else.

Two days before I was supposed to leave, there was a big networking event at a fancy restaurant on Las Olas Boulevard in Fort Lauderdale that had an outdoor garden. Joanie wanted me to go with her as her date while she mingled with her medical industry colleagues. I accepted the invitation, but my mind was on heading to England two days later. My future depended on it.

CHAPTER 26

The networking event was on a Tuesday evening. The weather was beautiful and I went to pick Joanie up at her house. She came out all dressed up and looking gorgeous as ever as she stepped into my car. This girl knew how to put herself together when she was going to an event. She had bright blue, sparkling Irish eyes and a very cute and sculptured face. Her hair was in a pixie cut and her earrings accentuated her cheekbones and her lips. She wore a gorgeous evening dress and high-heeled shoes that revealed her perfectly pedicured toes.

As I pulled into her driveway, she must have been looking out the window because she opened the door and came out. I immediately jumped out of the driver's seat, went around, and opened the door for her. She liked being treated like a lady although she was a real vamp. She smelled delicious. I was dressed up in a nice suit, had a suntan, and didn't look too bad myself. She told me how handsome I was and what a great looking couple we were.

As we drove away, we put on music, she held my hand softly, and we headed over to Las Olas Boulevard. When we got to the restaurant where the event was being held, I had the valet take the car and we went in.

It was a high-end networking event for medical professionals and it was clear she knew everyone in the room. She was vivacious and had a pretty good reputation in the medical field as a practicing RN and as someone who was well known in the medical billing industry. This was from working at the nautical training school with Stan.

No one questioned us, but we made it pretty clear that we were a couple. We were among the first ones there and as the room filled up, she went her way and I went my way, walking around talking to different people and picking on finger food that was all over the place. All the hors d'oeuvres were high-end: shrimp and lobster rolls, stuffed mushrooms, crab cakes, and all kinds of delectable gourmet food. More and more people showed up and by seven o'clock the place was packed. I didn't know anyone there, but was cordial as I made my way in and out between the bar and the outdoor tables.

Suddenly I noticed a very beautiful woman sitting with a guy at a high-top table. I went right past her and then turned around. I noticed that she was looking at me and as soon as I turned around to look back at her, I immediately felt electricity pass between us. She was absolutely stunning!

She looked just like Susan Sarandon and as I made my way back to her table, I said hello. She immediately took my hand and said, "Please, sit with us for a while."

She asked me my name and said her name was Lina; she was there with a guy who, when I got close, I could tell was clearly gay. He apparently did some graphic artwork for the medical industry and she just happened to be sitting with him.

When she started to speak, I could tell she was from New York. She actually sounded like Marisa Tomei in *My Cousin Vinny*. She had the whole New York thing going on.

She had straight black hair, beautiful facial structure, brown eyes and ruby red lips. The whole picture of her took my breath away. She was wearing a flowing dress and sandals. Her perfume filled my senses while I was close to her and I had an immediate, deep attraction that I didn't know what to do with. It was overwhelming and something I never had felt before, no matter how many women I had been with.

Joanie was walking around the room speaking to other people when she came upon me at Lina's table and said hello. I looked at her and said, "Oh, this is Joanie."

Lina extended her hand and Joanie shook it and said, "Well, I guess I better not interrupt you, John." I did not want to leave Lina, not even for a minute.

It was clear that Joanie was jealous and a little pissed. It was a good thing I asked Lina for her phone number just before I left the table. She wrote it on a napkin quickly and handed it to me just before Joanie got next to me. That was a close one.

I stuffed the napkin into my pocket and that was that. At least I could get in touch with her again. For the rest of the evening, Joanie was clearly upset that I was smitten by somebody other than her. She had no reason to, because she was with Stan and made no secret about it. In addition, she had other suitors and let me know very well when I was not allowed to go over to her house, based on who she had visiting her. Joanie liked to be in control, but as soon as I met Lina, she clearly was not.

For the rest of the evening, which only lasted another hour, Joanie was subdued. We sat at a table, had another drink, chatted with a few people, and then she said she wanted to go home because she was tired. On the way home she was quiet and said it was very rude of me to meet somebody else at an affair that she had invited me to.

I said I was just being friendly, but I knew very well I was about to embark on a whole new adventure and really wasn't sure what the outcome would be. As soon as we got to her house, I could tell she was more than a little mad. She jumped out of the car, closed the door, and told me not to worry about walking her to the door. She didn't even say good night. She just slammed the door and went inside.

As soon as I dropped Joanie off, I called Lina at the number she gave me. She immediately answered the phone because she had just gotten home herself. We talked on the phone from nine o'clock to eleven and even though I was very close to where I lived, I kept driving around and talking to her.

She worked for Sam's Club and was a transplant from Albany, New York, where she had grown up and lived her whole life. She was divorced and had just broken up with a guy and moved to Florida for a fresh start. She had dated a few guys since arriving, but at this time had no one special. At least that was what she told me. I could not stop talking to her and it seemed like we had a lot in common: our New York upbringing, ideology, mannerisms, voice inflections, and her whole persona. From the moment I met her, I felt that I was in love with her and that I'd known her my entire life!

As I talked to Lina, I told her I was leaving for England in two days. I explained everything about the company I had had, all the cruises I had gone on, the invention, and the fact that I was going to England because someone wanted to buy the invention and have me work with them as part of the patent deal.

She was impressed and I think she smelled money, but it seemed like she had done okay in her divorce settlement and that money wasn't her motive. I wasn't quite sure what her aim was, but I told her that when I returned, I would love to go on a date with her. She accepted right away and told me to call her when I got back.

The next day I was getting ready to leave. As soon as Kristen went to work at the police department, I called Joanie; she answered the phone on the first ring and said, "Oh, it's little Johnny. How is your new girlfriend today?"

I said, "Don't be silly. I just met her. I don't even know her. Besides that, what makes you think she's my girlfriend?"

She said, "I know you. I could tell by your eyes that you really liked her. I guess you don't like me anymore, do you?"

I said, "Of course I still like you. I just met that woman. I know nothing about her, so stop jumping to conclusions. And besides, you have Stan and all these other men in your life. You don't need me."

She said, "How do you know. Maybe I do?"

I said, "Well, I don't know. You know, you confuse me. One minute you want to be with me, the next minute you don't, and the next minute you're running over to Stan's house, then the next minute you have another guy you're going out with. So don't tell me about who wants to be with whom." With that, I told Joanie I had to get ready because I was leaving for England the next day from Miami International Airport at six PM.

That night I hardly slept. All I could think about was Lina and the feeling I had when I was around her. It totally consumed me and for some reason I felt that this was something that wasn't going to go away quickly. I didn't feel any overwhelming sexual attraction. I felt more of a deep connection on a spiritual level. I didn't even know this person, so how could this be possible?

She was very religious and said she went to church every Sunday. This was the first time I had ever felt anything like this with any woman I had ever been with. Wanting to go to bed with her was not at all the first thing on my mind. From the moment I met her, I felt she was the one I wanted to be with for the rest of my life. I don't know why, I couldn't explain it, but this is what I felt. I was completely captivated by everything about her.

I was halfway packed the next morning, had my passport, and had saved up $800 that I was going to take with me on the trip to England. I had the cash hidden in my underwear drawer. About six hours before I had to leave, I opened the drawer, looked where I had put the money, and— it was gone! I went crazy! I thought I had made a mistake. Maybe I had put it somewhere else? I looked all over the house but to no avail. It was gone.

Kristen came home from work and I was absolutely going out of my mind. I only had $65 cash on me and that was all the money I had. Kristen wasn't going to get paid for two more weeks and there was only about $60 left in the bank.

The only thing we could think of was that Sergio must have taken the money. I tried calling him several times and he didn't answer. About three o'clock, an hour before I had to be at the airport, he came home. His eyes were bloodshot and I could tell he was stoned.

I started screaming at him and asked him if he had taken my money. He said, "Who, me? I would never do that."

He wasn't very convincing and I knew he was lying. I started shaking him and screaming at him and told him it was the only money I had left to go to England with in order to try to get a deal to save our family!

He vehemently denied taking the money, but I was sure that he had done it. He started screaming back at me and then he stormed out of the house. I had no choice but to go to England with $65 in my pocket. I did not even have a return ticket because when I got to England the new company was going to buy me a ticket then, not knowing exactly what day I would return. They said Halloween, but it might have to be longer, so they said they would get me a ticket to come back to Fort Lauderdale when I was there.

They had arranged for a limousine to pick me up to take me to the Miami airport for my trip to Manchester. I said goodbye to Kristen. The guy put my suitcase in the trunk of the car and we were off.

In the car I called Joanie and said I was on the way. She asked me specifics about exactly what town I was going to be in and the name of the hotel. I was curious as to why she wanted so much detail. When I asked her why, she said, "You'll see, and you'll see me in England!" With that she hung up.

We got to the airport just in time. I got out of the car at the international terminal and checked in. I tried to call Lina, but got no answer, so I left a message.

Before you know it, I was boarding the plane and taking off to England. Something told me this was going to be a very interesting trip. I wasn't sure exactly what to expect and I was apprehensive about the future.

All I could say is that Joanie showed up in England and it was an incredibly wild week as I worked and we played, driving on the wrong side of the road, all over the English countryside.

When we got back to the United States, Joanie went her way and I went mine...but the story with Lina continued.

After all I had done, sailing on over 350 cruises around the world, making and losing millions of dollars, being with hundreds of women, having the fancy cars, houses, a 50 foot yacht, and everything else that money could buy, suddenly I was mentally and emotionally devoted to Lina. I thought this would never happen, but it did.

This concludes the story for now. Is it the end? By no means! It's only the beginning of an even more incredible journey that would traverse the United States from Florida to Graceland, Arizona, Carmel, Napa Valley and eventually Las Vegas, with Joanie following me, as well as many of the other women I had been with over the years. Even Kristen eventually settled in Las Vegas after she retired from the police department in Florida.

For the next twelve years, Lina was always in my heart and mind. She was truly the straw that broke the camel's back. You will never believe the rest of the story, but if you believe what I have just told you, there is no reason not to... "Never Enough Love" was really never enough, until that fateful night when my eyes met Lina's for the first time.

THE END FOR NOW

Printed in the United States
By Bookmasters